The LORD *in the* FIRES

Increasing in the Awe of God

James Maloney

WESTBOW®
PRESS
A DIVISION OF THOMAS NELSON
& ZONDERVAN

WestBow Press books may be ordered through booksellers or by contacting:

WestBow Press
A Division of Thomas Nelson & Zondervan
1663 Liberty Drive
Bloomington, IN 47403
www.westbowpress.com
1 (866) 928-1240

Unless otherwise noted, scripture taken from the New King James Version. Copyright © 1979, 1980, 1982 by Thomas Nelson, Inc. Used by permission. All rights reserved.

Scripture taken from the King James Version of the Bible.

ISBN: 978-1-4908-5561-5 (sc)
ISBN: 978-1-4908-5562-2 (hc)
ISBN: 978-1-4908-5563-9 (e)

Library of Congress Control Number: 2014918041

Printed in the United States of America.

WestBow Press rev. date: 11/21/2014

CONTENTS

"WHEREFORE GLORIFY YE THE LORD IN the fires, even the name of the Lord God of Israel in the isles of the sea." (Isaiah 24:15, KJV)

INTO THE FIRE

ISAIAH 24:15 IS ANOTHER ONE OF THOSE EXAMPLES OF why I prefer the King James Version over other translations—not that the other translations are *wrong*, but there's something extremely poignant and poetic about the phrase "the Lord in the fires."

"Therefore in the east give glory to the Lord" just kinda loses the oomph, in my opinion, though it is a correct rendering.

"Dawning light" is a little better, I suppose, especially with "isles of the sea" referring to the west. Basically, east to west, praise Him no matter what (see Malachi 1:11.) Yes, that's true. But fire also means fire (that's revelatory, huh?)

The Hebrew word *uwr* (Strong's #217) is pronounced something like "ore," and comes from the root *owr* (aren't you glad you don't have to speak ancient Hebrew?) That's the same word in Numbers 6:25, "The Lord make His face shine upon you, and be gracious to you..." The literal meaning is "flame, light;" metaphorically "to shine forth." So yes, it means the light of the sky (the sun rising from the east), but it also connotes revelation, something revealed by the light of the flame; as dross is brought to the surface by fire, what is pure is what remains. The burning away reveals the gold underneath, so to speak.

"I counsel you to buy from Me gold refined in the fire, that you may be rich..." (Revelation 3:18)

Therefore, glorify the Lord in the fires, see?

The context of Isaiah 24-27 is a long, poetical prophecy that outlines the catastrophes the Jews will go through, but it also shares the shining outcome of the gospel being preached throughout the world, and the ultimate victory of the Church, culminating in righteous peace forever. It isn't a pleasant experience, going through the fires, but the outcome is worth the purging. And that's something we're going to look at in this book.

"The fear of the Lord is the beginning of wisdom; a good understanding have all those who do His commandments. His praise endures forever." (Psalm 111:10)

I think many Christians have only a half-revelation concerning the "fear of the Lord." Yes, fear means fear (that's deep.) We'd be wise not to mess around concerning just how holy the Lord is. It really is true, the fear of the Lord is the beginning of wisdom and knowledge (Proverbs 1:7; 9:10.) There is an expectation on God's part that we approach Him with reverential worship, awe, and perhaps a touch of disquiet, and woe to those who treat that expectation with scorn and derision—that's just unwise. It isn't so much because we're afraid He's gonna blast us to atoms, but rather that we know *nothing* is hidden from Him. He's got us all figured out, and let's face it, He's holding all the cards. This is why He is God, and we are not. We can never forget that God is wholly "Other"—and while we are in His image, we are not of the exact same substance, are we? There is such a thing as healthy concern when facing omnipotent deity.

Like Peter points out, it is written: "Be holy, for I am holy." (1 Peter 1:16; Leviticus 44-45, et. al.) That's pretty clear, not any room for argument there. Since all of our righteousness is as filthy rags (Isaiah 64:6), that may seem like an unattainable concept: being holy. And in and of ourselves, it *is* impossible. This is one of the fundamental basics of human depravity, our inability to be justified before God in ourselves—pick the nicest, sweetest, kindest person on earth, and at some point in time they have done or thought something that makes them blamable before God.

Since God is perfectly holy, we must be perfectly holy in order to be accepted by Him. Our works can never save us (Ephesians 2:8); we know the just shall live by faith (Habakkuk 2:4; Hebrews 10:38), and yet, faith without works is dead. (James 2:17) If we believe all these things, how then can we reconcile God's commandment to be holy as He is?

Through faith in Christ, we can do all things (Philippians 4:13), even being holy. By Christ—who is God—taking our punishment for the sins of the entire world, and by us putting our trust in His redemptive works, we are filled with His life, His holiness, and His Spirit, thereby receiving acceptance and justification before the Lord God. And then through a process of yielding to the Spirit, now living inside us, we can begin to lead a holy life. Will we ever be completely without sin while living on this planet? No. But through a lifestyle of repentance and dying to self, we can lead a life that is holy (set apart) unto the Lord. One of the points of this book is to outline just how we do that by yielding to the Lord in the fires.

"Therefore, since we are receiving a kingdom which cannot be shaken, let us have grace, by which we may serve God acceptably with reverence and godly fear. For our God is a consuming fire." (Hebrews 12:28-29)

There it is again, fire. A consuming fire. This is our God, we mustn't forget this is who we serve. Remember that the Lord was described by John as having "eyes like a flame of fire." (Revelation 1:14) That's intense! This is our Savior, full of love and mercy, with eyes of burning flames!

The Lord gives us grace to be able to serve Him acceptably, with

3

reverence and a godly fear. From the outset of this book, we need to recognize that it is only by the gracing of the Holy Spirit working within us, as we yield to His fire, that we are able to receive the kingdom. This goes beyond our initial salvation experience, though that is of the utmost importance, but rather this book is intended to speak of our progression in the Lord.

We are not to remain as babes, only drinking the milk of the Word. No, we are to buy His gold, refined in fire. We are to burn with fervent zeal for an ever-increasing understanding of who He is, what He is about, what He expects from us. We are to increase in our awe of His majesty, His greatness, and His power. His desires must become our desires, His commandments must become our joy and pleasure to fulfill. Thankfully, His yoke is easy and His burden is light. (Matthew 11:30)

God never intended us to remain ignorant concerning His Person and expression—which is simply the manifestation of His power and majesty on the earthly plane through us, His sons and daughters. I have written hundreds of pages prior to this book, outlining several keys that I think are important in allowing the Spirit to condition us—indeed, to *try* us with His fire—so that we can be molded into walking, talking expressions of His power and mercy and grace to the world at large.

We are to be living epistles, known and read of men. (2 Corinthians 3:1-3) It takes a work of grace and a work of fire in our lives to get us to the point where our own identities are so buried in Christ (Romans 6:3-5; Colossians 2:12) that it is the manifestation of the Lord Himself through us as empty vessels.

I have tried to show that progression of work in *The Dancing Hand of God* and on into *The Panoramic Seer* and *Overwhelmed by the Spirit*. You don't need to have read those books to benefit from this one, but it doesn't hurt.

This book outlines one of the foremost factors in being "dead in Christ" so that He may shine forth, and it's not the most popular of topics, often overlooked because it is uncomfortable to think of our great Savior, our loving, merciful God as a consuming fire. And yet, He is.

"Take heed to yourselves, lest you forget the covenant of the Lord your God which He made with you, and make for yourselves a carved image in the form of anything which the Lord your God has forbidden you. For the Lord your God is a consuming fire, a jealous God." (Deuteronomy 4:23-24)

And there's fire once again. The Lord in the fires, His name is Jealous. No, I'm serious: "...for you shall worship no other god, for the Lord, whose name is Jealous, is a jealous God..." (Exodus 34:14) He's very resolute in protecting His name.

"For My name's sake I will defer My anger, and for My praise I will restrain it from you, so that I do not cut you off. Behold, I have refined you, but not as silver; I have tested you in the furnace of affliction. For My own sake, for My own sake, I will do it; for how should My name be profaned? And I will not give My glory to another." (Isaiah 44:9-11)

So, yes, there is that element of the "fear of the Lord." It is an actual, reverential fear—not so much of hellfire, but of entreating the Lord with the respect and reverence due to Him, even when we go through the "furnace of affliction," for it is to test us that we buy gold refined in fire, to draw out the dross, so that purity shines forth. Thus is His name, Jealous, preserved.

Okay, so that is one facet of the "fear of the Lord," and there are tons of books out there about this concept. But perhaps I can, through God's grace and prompting, throw another facet of shining light on this truth, bring another flame out of the fire, so to speak.

As with the other books previously mentioned, I've tried to share, hopefully with some success, how our revelation of God's nature directly affects the supernatural activity in our lives and ministries. Where something of God's character remains veiled in shadows, we are left with only half-truths, half-victories. It takes His light and His fire burning brightly, zealously, within us to uncover a true aspect of who God is, and this is what sets His supernatural power operating in our lives.

We can read all the rhetoric and theory we want. We can listen to a thousand sermons, attend a hundred conferences, and all of that is important; but if we don't have an encounter with God's divine nature, we're left with an incomplete concept of who He is, and it hinders the flow of His Spirit in our operation. I'm not putting down the rhetoric, theory, sermons, conferences in the slightest. I'm just saying there must be a divine revelation added to all that—an encounter with the Lord— to really "get it."

Our *awe* of Him must be continually increased in greater and greater levels. We must build and continue to build, so that we might *know* Him, His boundless riches, and His unfathomable ways, as He wills and desires to show us. (Isaiah 28:10; Romans 11:33; Ephesians 3:8; Philippians 3:10) One of these encounters is in the fires, though it's not something we like talking about in Christian circles. Because no one likes to go through the fires of testing—well, maybe *you* do, but *I* sure don't, and I don't think I'm the only one...

Except, when we're in the fires, it brings us to a place of awe—that worshipful reverence, that *fear,* being *overwhelmed* by the revelation of His Person that releases the miraculous experience, the healing, the wholeness, the completeness, that we are looking for.

That, to me, is the other half of the "fear of the Lord" that perhaps many Christians don't have a full understanding of—how the fear of the Lord brings us into a state of awe, shocked into the awareness of God's character and what He wants to do for us, with us, through us.

To be "shocked" is to be drawn into a state of astonishment, amazement, to stand beside ourselves, jolted, stunned, staggered, flabbergasted, even alarmed! If we had a true revelation of God's Person, this would be the only sane response. I don't think anyone could meet with an aspect of God and not have their pulse race, being moved into a startled state of disquiet, a certain sense of *unease*. That's not wrong to feel that way when faced with the awesome presence of the Creator. After all, "Who is like You, O Lord, among the gods? Who is like You, glorious in holiness, fearful in praises, doing wonders?" (Exodus 15:11)

And one of the ways He brings us into that state of awe is in the fires of testing. So that's why I like the KJV of Isaiah 24:15. We must learn to glorify the Lord in the fires. This is how we can increase in the awe of God. And it is in that state of awe that we manifest exactly what the Lord is wanting to share with His people and the world.

"In this you greatly rejoice, though now for a little while, if need be, you have been grieved by various trials, that the genuineness of your faith, being much more precious than gold that perishes, though it is tested by fire, may be found to praise, honor, and glory at the revelation of Jesus Christ..." (1 Peter 1:6-7)

LET HIM BE YOUR FEAR

ISAIAH 8 IS A KEY PASSAGE FOR THE COURSE OF THIS book. You and I are given for signs and wonders. (Verse 18) We're supposed to be a testament to the life and power of Jesus Christ pouring through us and out into a hurting world.

People turn to dead things (represented by "mediums and wizards, who whisper and mutter.") They are seduced by a dead spirit, see? (Really, a "dead spirit" is just a demonic spirit. Mediums aren't conjuring up the dead; they're conjuring up demons. They just don't know with whom they are conversing.)

It is up to us, or rather, Christ through us, to awaken people to an increase in the awe of God, so that it shocks them into a state of reverential fear. (This implies we have to increase in that awe and reverential fear for ourselves, obviously.)

The Lord is speaking through Isaiah with a "strong hand" (Verse 11)—that means, He's not kidding around here. This is serious. God's asking a rhetorical question here: why do people seek the dead on the behalf of the living? (Verse 19) Shouldn't they be seeking God for the answers? Well, duh.

But see, here's the deal: God through Isaiah is saying, if these worldly mutterers and whisperers, the folks who aren't seeking the living God, aren't speaking according to these words—that is, "to the law and to the testimony" (reference Verse 16)—there is "no light in them." (Verse 20)

Dark and dead. No fire. Not vibrant and bright and burning and alive. They are not yielded to the Lord in the fires. They have not experienced His light, they have not had an "awe" encounter with the Lord.

God tells Isaiah (and us), Don't be these people. (Verse 11) "Nor be afraid of their threats, nor be troubled." In other words, don't fear these kinds of dead, dark things. Rather:

"The Lord of hosts, Him you shall hallow; let Him be your fear, and let Him be your dread." (Isaiah 8:13)

"He will be as a sanctuary, but a stone of stumbling and a rock of offense to both the houses of Israel, as a trap and a snare to the inhabitants of Jerusalem. And many among them shall stumble; they shall fall and be broken, be snared and taken." (Isaiah 8:14-15)

This is an extremely strong passage of scripture. May I paraphrase? "Don't fear the whisperers and mutterers, the dead things, the dark things... Don't concern yourself with them. No, concern yourself with Me. I should be the One you're preoccupied with."

And this isn't such a "God is mad at everyone and hovering over that Smite button" (although there *is* an element of that to this passage.) But amidst all the stumbles and snares and traps and being broken, there is also the comfort of "I will wait on the Lord... and I will hope in Him." (Verse 17) There's a right way and a wrong way to approach God. Isaiah was doing it the right way.

"Humble yourselves in the sight of the Lord, and He will lift you up." (James 4:10)

That's what this book hopes to shed some light on: the right way. We will be tested, we will go through fires, but we need to have the right response toward it. That comes from increasing in the awe of God. Hallow Him, let Him be your "fear and dread" (in light of the New Testament revelation of the Spirit's help, and grace in Christ Jesus, of course.)

Now, let me share an experience with you.

THE DOOR WAS OPEN

A LITTLE WHILE BACK, THE LORD GRACED ME WITH AN open vision. I trust by this time, if you've read my previous works, you know a little bit about me, enough to know that I don't just flippantly make this stuff up off the top of my head. It would be pretty much the height of stupidity to write a book on the fear of the Lord and then just make junk up to sell a few books. I hope you understand my intent and my heart when I say I had an open vision. It is with reverential fear that I present this to you as accurately and realistically as possible, without embellishment or overhyping an experience in the Lord.

It's all the Lord anyway, not James Maloney. The whole point of this book is to show a decrease of self so that the Lord may shine through. So, while I do *not* have open visions every time I eat a bowl of cereal flakes or take a nap, the Lord *has* given me a grace in a prophetic seer operation, and I don't apologize for it. Trust me, I'm not the only one out there with these kinds of experiences. And trust me when I say that kind of operation also requires a certain amount of "going through the fires" as well. Most of you know me, at least a little bit, and you know I'm as human as the next, uh, human.

Nevertheless, the Lord graced me with an open vision. What I mean by that is I saw this with my own eyes, but I wasn't "bodily transported" to this vision. This wasn't a dream, I was awake, but this wasn't just like watching a movie either. It was external (not in my mind's eye) but I also felt like I was there, with sights, sounds, smells, touches, tastes. It's a little difficult to explain, but I was standing in this pavilion, and I knew this represented the tabernacle of the Lord.

I trust you're familiar with the earthly tabernacle, right? The Outer Court, the Holy Place, and the Most Holy Place, or the Holy of Holies. Read the first part of Hebrews 9 and the last five chapters of Exodus if you're not.

Okay, so this pavilion represented the Holy Place. It wasn't overly ornate and fancy, but it wasn't dirty or cheap either. Just sort of basic, functional. Oddly enough, though, it wasn't Old Testament time with a bunch of men in robes and Moses-beards watching sheep. There were a few hundred Christians seated here, maybe four hundred, and they were dressed modernly. Many, if not most of them, were in need of some kind of physical healing. I could see they were hurting: blind eyes, deaf ears, tumors, crippling diseases, just a whole mess of humanity waiting in this pavilion. I could sense they were eagerly anticipating ministry for their healing.

I knew behind us was the Outer Court, down a set of steep steps. I thought there were people out there as well. Outside there was light. Sunshine. It was warm and nice. Inside the Holy Place, it was lit by tall lampstands that emanated warm light. Showbread always present, an alter of incense that was almost intoxicating; and it was nice here in the Holy Place, too, don't misunderstand me; but the people were still sick and suffering. And I found that strange. This was the tabernacle of God, and these were His people, yet many were still suffering. My heart longed for them to be made whole.

An angel appeared and escorted me between the wall of the pavilion and a row of seated people, up to the front where two flaps made a veil separating the Holy Place from the Most Holy Place. Another angel was standing beside one of the flaps, and these two cherubim reached out and lifted them up.

A warm flood of light filled the Holy Place, a wave of indescribable glory emanating out of the Holy of Holies, darkening the light of the lampstands, even the sunshine in the Outer Court, and the people oohed and ahhhed, basking in the glow. It felt really good, just to have that level of glory upon us. Some people were improved, but they weren't healed. Yet they seemed content just to sit in this level of imminence with God, absorbing a portion of His power, but they made no motion to go beyond the lifted veil.

The angels beckoned for us all to enter into the Most Holy Place, inviting us to go deeper. They seemed saddened that all of us weren't *rushing* to get into the Most Holy Place. Here they were, opening the doors, and the people just sat enraptured by the warm rays spilling out, not wanting to go in. Were they scared? Maybe. Did they feel unworthy? Perhaps. But mostly I think they were weighed down by dullness, a lack of understanding that lured them into complacency. I'm not minimizing their experience, but that level of encounter with God wasn't enough to see them completely set free; and there was no excuse, the invitation to enter was for *everyone*, come on in. Meet the Source of this glorious light.

I said to myself, "What, are you kidding me? Of *course* I'm going in there." So I walked toward the open flaps, and only three other people went with me. One was a man with a cane, dragging his leg as he shuffled forward. Another was a woman utilizing a walker. The last was a man in a wheelchair.

The moment we passed beyond the veil into the Most Holy Place, words fail me to properly describe the overwhelming awesome presence that bowled us over. In this Place, the light wasn't from lampstands, wasn't even from the sun. It was from the *shekinah* glory of the Lord

God. While I did not see the Father on the throne, I saw four-and-twenty elders who were worshipping Him. And I did see bolts of fiery lightning followed by crashing thunder, the sounds of trumpets, royal tapestries beyond human description arrayed in colors that cannot be replicated on earth. And everywhere were lights, shafts and beams of glory emanating from the Father of lights Himself. Waves of His glory rolled over us and we were fully immersed in the single greatest renewing experience I've ever had. It was energizing! Almost like God's love and *zoe* life were given visible form in the waves of light that washed over us. And then the shockwave hit us. We were bowled over, slain in the Spirit, made like dead men. The anointing, the reverence was almost too much to handle.

We basked in the unrestrained glory of God for a few minutes, and then I staggered back to my feet. The angels re-opened the flaps, letting some of that fire and heat escape back out into the Inner Court. When I exited the Holiest Place, I saw all the people anticipating for me to minister to them, to somehow express the glory I'd just witnessed to them vicariously. It's as if they *wanted* to experience the glory of God, but from a distance. I was reminded of Exodus 33, when Moses and Joshua went into the tabernacle, and every man stood at his tent door (Verse 8)—they themselves didn't want to go forward and enter in; they were content to get it secondhand from Moses.

So these people in the Holy Place were blessed, yes, but it was in a measure. And the angel led me past them down to the steep steps that led to the Outer Court, where I found maybe fifteen or twenty people waiting down by the curb. These were mostly unchurched, unsaved—cripples, blind and deaf folks who had been drawn to the tabernacle, attracted to God but not yet stepping into the Holy Place. The angel told me to minister to them, and I did. It was just an amazing expression of God's power and love. The demonized were delivered, all manner of physical need was healed, whatever they were struggling under didn't matter—the Lord's grace was sufficient for them all. They were saved and baptized in the Spirit and began praising God as their physical infirmities were healed. It was so awesome seeing wonderful breakthroughs and salvations, but in the back of my mind, I still felt sad for the few hundred Christians in the Holy Place.

When I was finished ministering, the angel led me back inside, past the waiting Christians, and the flaps were opened a second time, once again inviting everyone to enter. As the door was drawn back, I saw the cane fly out, followed by the walker, and lastly the lone wheelchair was pushed out, empty.

It was then I came out of the vision, both exhilarated, praising God as His power came over me, and yet also disheartened that so many of the people remained in the Holy Place but went no farther.

See, *those* kinds of miracles only took place in the Holy of Holies. I am convinced this is where it's coming to: people *must* come boldly into the Most Holy Place for themselves. (Hebrews 4:16) Jesus has rent the veil that separated us from God's very throne room, but most Christians seem reluctant to enter all the way in. I maintain that the majority of *these* kinds of miracles will happen in the Holy of Holies, where the fullness of glory is manifest, where we are intimate with the Father's imminence.

We are coming into an era of time very quickly—and I believe it will start with church leadership first—where God demands that His people press beyond the veil of flesh and enter into His Holiest Place in order to see the greater works, the greater expressions, the greater miracles. Not to downplay the measures of experiences we've had thus far, but the Lord will not share His glory with another. We will have to come up to Him at His level, beyond the sunlight of the Outer Court, beyond the light of the lampstands, and into the very fire of the throne room.

It's there that we will be changed from glory to glory; and as a word of admonition, if He can't get His people to come in, He'll open the back door and reach out to the people of the world with healing and displays of His power. That is a stark, amazing contrast! And potentially a little sad, but do not fear—you will see the Lord in all of His fiery glory!

You and I will enter the Holiest Place, and we will see those kinds of miracles, the rolling wheelchairs and all. Yes, there is blessing and grace and a measure of God's presence and anointing in the Holy Place— don't misunderstand my intention here—but we *have* to press all the way through if we want to experience the complete, total manifestation of God's power.

That scares a lot of well-meaning Christians, as it scared the Israelites at Mt. Sinai. (Exodus 20:19) But note Moses' response to them: "'...Do not fear; for God has come to test you, and that His fear may be before you, so that you may not sin.'" (Exodus 20:20)

Do not fear, but let *His* fear be before you. There is a right fear and a wrong fear, and only Moses drew near the thick darkness where God was.

Let's not be like the Israelites in Numbers 13-14. Yes, God pardoned their iniquity but it was at the expense of not seeing His glory fully revealed—they didn't enter into their inheritance. Oh sure, they'd seen measures of it in Egypt, in the wilderness, and nevertheless tempted the Lord "these ten times" (Numbers 14:22) with their murmurings and complainings, their evil report that marginalized God, implying He couldn't protect them from the giants in the land. How sad!

But I want to be one who has this right kind of fear. That's the point of this book. We are all servants, but God wants us to be *sons*. Sons are chastened, that's true, but they have a better understanding of it, as opposed to servants. Sons fear displeasing the father; servants fear the whipping rod.

There is always a remnant of those who press in harder than others, who utilize their rights in Christ Jesus to access the throne room and behold the all-consuming fire of our God. I want to be one of those people because it is here that the ultimate expression of His power and might and grace will be found. That expression comes at a cost, going through the fires as it were, but it is vital and necessary if we want to see the Lord in an ever-increasing measure.

I want this book to be a further catalyst for those people who are willing to pay any price, go through any fire, to experience more of their God.

That was my introduction. *smile* So let's begin.

Restoring the Spirit of Intimacy

IBELIEVE THERE IS A CRY IN THE HEARTS OF MANY OF God's people, a tenacious desire to come up higher in Him. I'm all about revival, and God coming down to His people, but I think it's a two-way street. God wants us to come up to Him! There is an unyielding passion and a thirsting to see God in a way few have seen before. I maintain it is in the spirit of intimacy that the understanding of the availability of God is restored to His people. Like the Psalmist said, "So I have looked for You in the sanctuary, to see Your power and Your glory." (Psalm 63:2)

One primary way we restore that spirit of intimacy is in the fires, the pressings and testings of the Holy Spirit. Adversity forces us to draw closer to the Lord, our great Comforter.

Paul's declaration needs to be our own:

"But what things were gain to me, these I have counted loss for Christ. Yet indeed I also count all things loss for the excellence of the knowledge of Christ Jesus my Lord, for whom I have suffered the loss of all things, and count them as rubbish, that I may gain Christ and be found in Him, not having my own righteousness, which is from the law, but that which is through faith in Christ, the righteousness which is from God by faith; **that I may know Him and the power of His resurrection, and the fellowship of His sufferings, being conformed**

to His death, if, by any means, I may attain to the resurrection from the dead.

"Not that I have already attained, or am already perfected; but I press on, that I may lay hold of that for which Christ Jesus has also laid hold of me.

"Brethren, I do not count myself to have apprehended; but one thing I do, forgetting those things which are behind and reaching forward to those things which are ahead, I press toward the goal for the prize of the upward call of God in Christ Jesus." (Philippians 3:7-14, **emphasis added**)

This is one of the greatest needs in the body of Christ: to *know* Him, the power of His resurrection, and the fellowship of His sufferings. We often ignore this aspect of Christianity, and that's not a critical statement, because it is human nature to want to avoid adversity whenever possible. It's built within us to want things to be "easy"—and that's not necessarily wrong. But as pertains to the knowledge of Christ, and thus the power of His resurrection (which is our means and ways to obtain *anything* that we are in need of from the Father) requires a fellowship with His sufferings. Not that we find attainment in those sufferings—absolutely not!—for Christ's sacrifice was sufficient for anything we lack, anything at all. And yet, the "fellowship" with those sufferings (not go through them yet again) is an important part of our growth in the Lord.

We must come to a state of dissatisfied satisfaction, if I can phrase it that way, a certain restlessness in the "rest" of the Holy Spirit (see Hebrews 4.) A burning desire to press beyond the veil of our flesh, as it were; to be consumed with His zeal.

As Jesus said so eloquently, "Unless you eat the flesh of the Son of Man and drink His blood, you have no life in you." (See John 6:53-58.)

I've said elsewhere that one must really *eat and drink* of the Son of

Man; I mean in a devouring, ravenous, unrestrained manner—like a starving man. Not just a neat nibble here and there, you know? That's not *eating*. That's tasting. But what we're talking about, in the fires, is *eating*. That is what it means to be consumed with zeal for the Lord. We must come up higher!

Our cry needs to be John 14:8: "Lord, show us the Father..." Now, look, Philip's heart was in the right place, but his revelation was lacking. Notice the Lord's response to him: "Have I been with you so long, and yet you have not known Me, Philip? He who has seen Me has seen the Father; so how can you say, 'Show us the Father'? Do you not believe that I am in the Father, and the Father in Me?" (Verses 9-10)

We know that everything is centered in Christ, but it takes Christ, through the Spirit (and yes, through the fires, even) to give us that true revelation of the Father. To really know His heart, His desires, and even His wants. I know the Father is in *need* of nothing, but His purpose and desires must become our purpose and desires. This is why intimacy is so important (and so costly.)

This revelation comes at a price, but this is why I love miracles so much. I'll never understand why Christians, most of them well-meaning, downplay the miraculous as "superfluous" in this day and age, as if it it's something unnecessary.

A miracle is the act of God's power displaying His perfect character, His mighty and divine faculties. Why in the world would a Christian not want that? Miracles impel us *toward* Him—we are *staggered* into an awareness and brought into a state of wonderment, astonishment; truly, we increase in the awe of God through miraculous encounters. To say the age of miracles has passed cuts God off at the knees, so to speak.

Rather, I believe it is because they *fear* the price that comes from perceiving the supernatural. They don't want to pay the price that witnessing a miracle requires of them. They fear the fires.

But that's just what most of us need! We need a greater revelation of the Person of God. Who He is. *Charisma* is simply an expression of who He is—not something He can do. It is the manifestation of His very character on the earthly plane.

We need a Damascus Road experience! (Acts 9) Here's Saul, right, breathing threats and murders against the disciples of Jesus. A bolt of light, a shaft of heavenly fire, zaps him, knocking him down. And he's on the ground, trembling and astonished, when the voice of the Lord calls out to him, "Why are you harassing Me? You sure are a dumb ox!" Okay, I'm paraphrasing, but that's what "kick against the goads" means. It's a Greek proverb basically saying, "Don't be stupid," because a stubborn plow ox would kick back against the driver's prod, digging the spur deeper into the flesh.

Saul's response isn't, "My goodness, what a strange experience I've just had. I say, what is this lightning bolt that's struck me?" Rather, he's all, "Who *are* You? Lord?!" as if to say, "My God, You're who I've been railing against?" Why, that *is* rather like a dumb ox, ain't it?

We too, like Paul, can be stunningly "ox-like," can't we? I know I'm not the only one, don't smirk at me. It takes the fires from heaven to awaken us into a certain level of understanding of just *who* Christ is—our God and Maker, our Herd Driver, as it were—and we'd be very wise not to kick against the cattle prod, you know? That's a great way to get zapped!

"The glory of the Lord shall be revealed, and all flesh shall see it together; for the mouth of the Lord has spoken." (Isaiah 40:5)

Look, the Lord *is* healing, the Lord *is* moving miraculously, whether we want Him to or not. He permits Himself to reveal His character to the world—to *boast* in Himself, since He will not give that glory to another. (Isaiah 42:8) Not with us, not with any carved image, no one. So, if this is true (and it is, sorry) then we only hurt ourselves by denying the expression. And we hurt others, too, because if we are *seeing* it, then we are changed by it (it cannot be helped—fire consumes, no matter what!), and you will not be dissuaded in *sharing* it with others.

As I've said in other works, we know that everywhere Jesus went, He perfectly and completely manifested the reputation of the Father into reality. (Hebrews 1:3, and again John 14:9) God's glory is simply His reputation on display, and reputation is simply an opinion of a person's worth.

I believe we are being charged with a heavenly dynamic to manifest a visible, audible, tangible expression of God's worth to the world. We do *not* serve a dumb idol! We have a faithful High Priest (Hebrews 2:17)—and our availability to God through Him is the key to coming up higher. God wants fellowship with mankind; He wants His reputation resting on us, and I will keep asking this question again and again: Will you allow God's reputation to be seen in you?

Of course that comes at a price, but we have not gone through anything that our High Priest has not gone through (Hebrews 4:15)—apart from sin, that is. Concerning this availability of God, never forget that He apprehended you first. God will *always* take the first step, even in the fires (see Exodus 3:1-6, the bush *was* burning.) When you came to Him, you just chose what He had already chosen for you to enter into in the first place—this is the same for the miraculous as for salvation.

(I'm not being ultra-Calvinistic here—I simply mean, the Lamb was slain from the foundation of the world [Revelation 13:8], and salvation—and the miraculous—is available to any and all who would choose it, and who are willing to pay the price.)

One of the greatest truths in Christianity is the revelation that God makes Himself available, and in turn, we must make ourselves available, for salvation *and* for that kind of experiential knowledge we're talking about in the release of the miraculous.

I've used John, one of the Sons of Thunder, as an example before (see John 13:23.) It is a truth that Jesus loved all of His disciples equally, yet John availed himself of Christ's availability, even though prior he was not known as some great lover of God or of people. John made himself available and those "love encounters" with Christ changed him from a raging man into the apostle of love. That's miraculous, folks! We need love embraces, we need hug therapy. The Lord will transform us as He transformed John by meeting the "unmet love needs" of His followers.

This is why the miraculous is so important, and a spirit of continual, deepening intimacy with Him, God wants us to have a love encounter with Him. This is hard for a lot of people. This is a "fire" in and of itself. But a necessary, vital one, so suck it up. We can't give out what we haven't received because we are not the originators of love, only recipients. And if we haven't received it, we can't give it.

"By this we know love, because He laid down His life for us. And we also ought to lay down our lives for the brethren." (1 John 3:16)

Remember, the miraculous is focused love.

Fall on Your Neck

"AND HE AROSE AND CAME TO HIS FATHER. BUT WHEN he was still a great way off, his father saw him and had compassion, and ran and fell on his neck and kissed him." (Luke 15:20)

Have you permitted the Father to *fall* on your neck and kiss you? I might have pointed this out before, but I'll do it again, since it's appropriate: "While Peter was still speaking these words, the Holy Spirit **fell** upon all those who heard the word." (Acts 10:44, **emphasis added**) Same Greek word. The miraculous expression is rooted in love. Let the Spirit fall upon you! Be a receiver, and an expresser, of love. Be a love messenger. To the extent one receives and expresses love, it can be said that one knows God! (1 John 4:8)

Every prophecy, every healing, every deliverance, every revelation is a love embrace. And we say miracles are no longer needed in this day and age? No wonder everyone is lacking in love.

Hey, look, I believe in biblical indoctrination, being grounded in the Word; I honor educators of the Word, because I *are* one. I fully support that we must study and know the Bible, and apply it, you know? But indoctrination doesn't always change you... It takes a work of the Spirit alongside it. And that is miraculous, that is *fire*.

"Nevertheless when one turns to the Lord, the veil is taken away. Now the Lord is the Spirit; and where the Spirit of the Lord is, there is liberty. But we all, with unveiled face, beholding as in a mirror the glory of the Lord, are being transformed into the same image from glory to glory, just as by the Spirit of the Lord." (2 Corinthians 3:16-18)

Glory to glory, we are changed into the *same image*. Every miracle and healing restores intimacy with God's abilities. Every revelation and deliverance restores intimacy with God's purity. And every word of prophecy restores intimacy with God's voice. And we say we have no need of the apostolic and the prophetic in today's "community-reaching" church? Who are we trying to kid here? Not the people out *there*, I guarantee you. The world needs a love embrace.

I think many of us need deliverance from a fear of approaching God. That's the wrong kind of fear from what we're talking about in this book, and it is a work of fire to burn that wrong kind of fear to the ground. Shame and condemnation must be burnt away. And dare I say, the same for legalism—even sensuality. It all must go in the fires.

Because God wants fellowship, on a higher level than He has even now. How many scriptures talk about God wanting to commune with mankind?

"You are worthy, O Lord, to receive glory and honor and power; for You created all things, and by Your will they exist and were created." (Revelation 4:11) Here's another instance of a "better" translation found in the original King James: "and for thy pleasure they are and were created." That means He *wants* us around. He takes pleasure in having us created (we're included in "all things.")

"And they heard the sound of the Lord God walking in the garden in the cool of the day, and Adam and his wife hid themselves from the presence of the Lord God among the trees of the garden. Then the Lord God called to Adam and said to him, 'Where are you?'" (Genesis 3:8-9)

And yet, it must be fellowship on His terms, because He is holy. If you don't believe me, read Exodus 32.

"'Because they ministered to them before their idols... they shall not come near Me to minister to Me as priest, nor come near any of My holy things, nor into the Most Holy Place; but they shall bear their shame and their abominations which they have committed.'" (Ezekiel 44:12-13)

But those who come to Him on His terms, He invites to fellowship with Him.

"'But the priests, the Levites, the sons of Zadok, who kept charge of My sanctuary when the children of Israel went astray from Me, they shall come near Me to minister to Me; and they shall stand before Me to offer to Me the fat and the blood,' says the Lord God." (Ezekiel 44:15)

Let's be sons of Zadok, okay? God wants us to experience a love that *possesses* us! We know that God so loved the world He sent His only begotten Son, right? But did you know there is a greater, deeper love than John 3:16? No, really. It goes beyond His love for the whole world; He wants to actually *abide* with us, each of us individually—that's one of the benefits of being omnipresent, there's enough of Him to go around for everyone on the planet as a singular person. Here's the Lord's take on this concept:

"'He who has My commandments and keeps them, it is he who loves Me. And he who loves Me will be loved by My Father, and I will love him and manifest Myself to him.'

"Judas (not Iscariot) said to Him, 'Lord, how is it that You will manifest Yourself to us, and not to the world?'

"Jesus answered and said to him, 'If anyone loves Me, he will keep My word; and My Father will love him, and We will come to him and make Our home with him.'" (John 14:21-23)

Think about that, God Almighty will make His home with you. Remember, this conversation in John 14 began with, "In My Father's house are many mansions [dwellings]." (Verse 2) Jesus went on to say the Father dwelled in Him. (Verse 13) He then speaks of the indwelling Spirit (the Helper) so that we are not left orphans, because we have a home with the Spirit sharing space with us. (Verses 17, 18)

That Greek word for "make Our home" in Verse 23 stems from the root *meno* (Strong's #3306, "MAY-no"), and it means "to sojourn, abide, tarry; to not depart; to last, endure, and not perish; to hold and keep continually; to remain as one."

All that God promises us is Himself forever! And what a promise! You know, the Promised Land for the Israelites was just *bait* used to lure them into something even more wonderful: God Himself dwelling with them always!

All these love embraces we're talking about, the expression of the miraculous, are there to lead us into a relationship with Him—not just our own inherited Canaan. The point of the supernatural is not the end result, it is the stepping stone toward something greater: relationship with God. God speaks and moves miraculously in order to have fellowship with us, and then (secondly) to train, to teach, and to reveal to us. See the distinction? The Word (and the Spirit) point to the Father, but there is a place of intimacy with God that is deeper even than what the Bible shows us—in the heavenly realm, as we come up higher. Note, I'm not saying this does *away* with the Word—rather, the Word goes beyond itself as just merely the printed page and points us to vibrant intimacy. Let's phrase it this way: there is a place where you will be able to hear the Word *from* Him, not just *about* Him.

Very few of us (and I include myself in that "us") are at a place of such depth and familiarity with God Himself. In most cases—and this is not a critical statement—everything has enlarged in our lives (our biblical knowledge, our understanding of spiritual concepts, perhaps even our demonstration of the supernatural)—except God. Many times, we serve the Lord deeply, in whom we don't know deeply. Selah.

So this presents questions: What are we going to do as priests unto God? Are we a God-person? Are we concerned with *Him*, not just what's *His*, if that makes sense? What I mean by that is, are we concerned with His delights, desires, and "wants"? That's what it means to be a God-person. Are we involved, affected by and relating to *His* concerns and motivations? I mean, something we desire can seem like "just what we need" on the surface—we might cry out, "Give us Your power, Lord!"—and that's not wrong, but it might not really be what needs to be imparted to us. Perhaps it's more love, or more patience, or endurance, tempering, whatever. Some kinds of pursuits, while honorable from one standpoint, can be surface—not true intimacy with what truly matters to God, and that should be what consumes us: finding out what *He* wants.

Are we coming up higher? We cannot be satisfied with the obvious, surface truth. Something can sound good, look good, but what about the real *meat* underneath the skin? Getting down to the so-called brass tacks. God wants *multitudes* flocking to Him with unbridled ferocity— the *violent* who take it by force, shaking the status quo of everyone surrounding them.

God's heart's cry is, Give Me men and women of communication! Those that would hear from Me! Jesus wants you to know Him in the kind of relationship where you hear Him talk about Himself to you.

"So the Lord spoke to Moses face to face, as a man speaks to his friend. And he would return to the camp, but his servant Joshua the son of Nun, a young man, did not depart from the tabernacle." (Exodus 33:11)

Let's go back to the Israelites in Exodus 32. Remember they broke off their golden earrings to make the calf, right? Their sin? It wasn't *just* in the broadest sense. What they were guilty of was they didn't see their *need* for Him.

They didn't see Him bringing them back into a face-to-face relationship with Himself. Oh, sure, they had a lusting for *knowledge*— remember, it does say in Exodus 33:8, that when Moses was going to talk to the Lord face-to-face, each man came and stood at his tent door to watch him. Don't tell me they weren't interested in the concept of someone speaking with God as a friend. "…Always learning and never able to come to the knowledge of the truth." (2 Timothy 3:7) Like Adam and Eve trading the Tree of Life for the knowledge of good and evil. Content with a concept of God, some golden calf, and not the real Person. Constantly chasing after ideas, and not arriving at the Originator of ideas. This is how they fell short of the glory of God.

Like in the vision earlier, content with the Holy Place, but very few (just Moses in this case) concerned with the Holy of Holies. You can know the Word of God and still don't want His presence. Think about that.

Jesus said He was the Way, the Truth, and the Life. (John 14:6) The Way is the Outer Court, the Truth is the Inner Court, but it is the *Life* that is found in the Holiest Place.

It is in the Holiest Place that the shekinah glory resides. That word is akin to *shakan*, check out the Hebrew (see Strong's #7931, "SHAH-can.") It means "to settle down, to abide, to dwell, to reside." God wants His glory (His reputation and His character, the extension of His divine Person) to be a housemate with you, a life-long companion, a lover, really. If you want to delve deeply, the primitive root connotes the idea of lodging together, and in reality means to "lay with," as a husband and wife will lay together, not to put too fine a point on it. (See Strong's #7901.) It can mean "to lie on." Ahem. I'll let you figure out the rest. We're talking about an intimate relationship here, folks.

God's people need to have an "awe" encounter with their Lover, you see. If we truly had an understanding of what it means to be the Bride of Christ, our Groom. Well, it's a shakan kind of relationship, isn't it? That's why God calls idolatry "harlotry." Giving yourself to another in a way God wants you only for Himself. He wants to be One with His Bride, and He is Jealous. He will not share His glory with another—so don't play around.

Yes, there is a fire; and yes, there is a right fear of the Lord; and yet, wouldn't you like to be a Moses? The alternative:

"'These words the Lord spoke to all your assembly, in the mountain from the midst of the fire, the cloud, and the thick darkness, with a loud voice; and He added no more. And He wrote them on two tablets of stone and gave them to me.

"'So it was, when you heard the voice from the midst of the darkness, while the mountain was burning with fire, that you came near to me, all the heads of your tribes and your elders. And you said: "Surely the Lord our God has shown us His glory and His greatness, and we have heard His voice from the midst of the fire. We have seen this day that God speaks with man; yet he still lives. Now therefore, why should we die? For this great fire will consume us; if we hear the voice of the Lord our God anymore, then we shall die. For who is there of all flesh who has heard the voice of the living God speaking from the midst of the fire, as we have, and lived? You go near and hear all that the Lord our God may say, and tell us all that the Lord our God says to you, and we will hear and do it."

"'Then the Lord heard the voice of your words when you spoke to me, and the Lord said to me: "I have heard the voice of the words of this people which they have spoken to you. They are right in all that they have spoken. Oh, that they had such a heart in them that they would fear Me and always keep all My commandments, that it might be well with them and with their children forever!"'" (Deuteronomy 5:22-29)

Let's be Moses.

THE KAIROS MIRACLE

L ET'S JUXTAPOSE SUBJECTIVE INSIGHT TO OBJECTIVE truth for just a second to lay down some groundwork for this next section. Any subjective experience, if it's truly initiated by the Spirit, is an important, even vital, part of developing a proper "awe" mentality in the fear of the Lord. In fact, most of the fires we go through are subjective experiences that the Spirit can use to teach us the importance of intimacy with God. Nevertheless, no subjective experience can take away or add to known clear, concise scripture.

"For I testify to everyone who hears the words of the prophecy of this book: If anyone adds to these things, God will add to him the plagues that are written in this book..." (Revelation 22:18)

With that being said, now that the rule is spelled out, I want to highlight a couple kingdom principles which will help us increase in the awe of God. It is from our understanding being enlightened (Ephesians 1:18) through experiential knowledge, subjected to the Word, that our intimacy with the Lord is increased. The Scriptures are illuminated by Spirit-led subjective experiences, in other words.

The Now Principle is something we need to understand, not just as a concept, but as an experience in God, an application of a physical truth—the same as gravity or inertia. We know the concept of gravity from school, but we *know* gravity works because we experience it firsthand. See what I mean?

Going through the fires of testing can help us have a practical, working knowledge of God's "nowness." We must be made to understand the exact closeness of God in the present. What I mean by that is, God is in the infinite *now*—the ever-present realm, living in the past, present and future simultaneously as just "now."

Many of us have a half-formed, incorrect notion of God being removed from the imminent scene—oh, sure, we may have some vague theory that God is "everywhere," because if He wasn't, He wouldn't be God. But in practice, a lot of well-meaning Christians, especially when faced with adversity and trials, tend to remove God to some distant place up in heaven, sitting upon a throne and peering down at us through the clouds. Remember that stupid song "From a Distance God is Watching Us" or whatever it was called. Yeah, that's not true actually.

The kingdom of heaven is at hand (Matthew 10:7 and others), which means it's now. It's nigh. It's here, not there. That is to say, the eternal realm of heaven has broken into our natural flow of time, and it is here, right now, just now. It's always here, right now, at this moment as you read these words.

You're probably aware of two different Greek words signifying "time"—*kairos* and *chronos*. (Strong's #2540 and #5550, "KAI-ros" and "CRO-nos," where all the "o's" are long) If not, chronos is calendar time: seconds, hours, days, weeks, months, years. Kairos is an act of God intervening at some juncture of chronos. A season of "special time." Chronos is bound to this earthly realm, which we can perceive as the passage of time. It's Saturday, not Sunday. It's March, not December. It's evening, not morning. And yet kairos is for the *now*, in the present. So the age of grace (the kairos of salvation) is *now*, because the kingdom of heaven is now. Make sense?

Being lodged in the chronos and putting the kairos off into the future can be a stronghold of the mind that many of us struggle against. It becomes a hindrance to increasing in the awe of God.

"For though we walk in the flesh, we do not war according to the flesh. For the weapons of our warfare are not carnal but mighty in God for pulling down strongholds, casting down arguments and every high thing that exalts itself against the knowledge of God, bringing every thought into captivity to the obedience of Christ, and being ready to punish all disobedience when your obedience is fulfilled." (2 Corinthians 10:3-6)

This stronghold, or mind-blinder, or whatever we wish to term it, keeps us bound to the past, living in the way of how things *were* ("Remember back in the '70s when God did such and such?"), or keeping us shackled to past disappointments and failures. Or it keeps us bound to the future, thinking, "Someday, eventually, it will happen," be that a breakthrough or a healing or whatever. Good things will happen *tomorrow* but not *right now.*

Living in an ever-increasing awe with God helps us keep "here and now" alive. God wants us to receive sooner rather than later, you know? And again, we may understand this as a vague theory, yet our actions and lifestyles proclaim a shackling to the past or to the future, instead of the "now."

Of course on the earth we are bound in time; yes, we have flesh-and-bone bodies, I recognize this. And yet, our spirit man, the essence of who we really are, is an eternal being, made in the image of God, that is simply "now." Our job, as we go through the fires, as we work with the Spirit, is to access the spirit man, going beyond our mind, our way of thinking. This is the "casting down" part of 2 Corinthians 10. Bringing every thought into captivity. Subjecting the flesh to the spirit in order to access the eternal realm of glory.

"And do not be conformed to this world, but be transformed by the renewing of your mind, that you may prove what is that good and acceptable and perfect will of God." (Romans 12:2)

It is the renewing of the mind that helps to shut down the noise, so to speak, of being trapped in the chronos. Why, we need to be transfigured after a fashion.

In Matthew 17, we read of the Lord being transfigured before Peter, James and John. I'm sure you know the passage. Here's Elijah and Moses (signifying the law and the prophets, of course) standing beside our Lord in His glorified state. The Father speaks out of heaven, the disciples hit the dirt—talk about an "awe" moment, right?

And yet, in the same chapter, we see a man begging the Lord to administer deliverance to his son, who was "moonstruck" (epileptic.) The disciples were unable to cure the child. Jesus laments, "How long must I bear this faithless generation?" and He rebuked the demon, healing the boy.

So the disciples later ask Him, "Why could we not cast it out?"

And Jesus, not one to ever pull any punches, says, "Because of your unbelief." And yes, I know He also says, "This kind does not go out except by prayer and fasting." But the principle remains the same in the context of our subject here: Jesus had an expectation for healing in the *now*. He perceived the kairos time intercepting that moment, and His faith in the God of that now-moment released the child. The fires of "prayer and fasting" (casting down, again) further solidified our Lord's stance that healing comes from an understanding of the kingdom of heaven being a "now" kingdom—it *is* at hand.

"But Jesus answered them, 'My Father has been working until now, and I have been working.'" (John 5:17)

And obviously Peter and John came to an understanding of the nowness of God because we see in Acts 3 the lame man was healed.

Peter read the nowness of the moment and the man was immediately made whole.

What I want to bring out here is that the disciples who saw the Lord transfigured were also "transfigured" in the workings of their mind. A revelation of just Who they were working for, and with, was added to their spiritual makeup. That, indeed, the kingdom of heaven was "now"—Elijah (John the Baptist) had already come and prepared the way, and now here was the Lord bringing heaven with Him. They were able to access that kairos understanding because of the experience they shared on the mount, whereas the disciples who had not seen the Lord transfigured were still struggling in actualizing that the kingdom of heaven was at hand, at least concerning the moonstruck boy.

What I'm saying is most miracles are from the created times of kairos, these appointed times spliced into the chronos of our day-to-day lives. When we come to an understanding that it is all in the infinite "now" of God, we can perceive what God is wanting to do in the *now*.

"But this people has a defiant and rebellious heart; they have revolted and departed. They do not say in their heart, 'Let us now fear the Lord our God, who gives rain, both the former and the latter, in its season. He reserves for us the appointed weeks of the harvest.'" (Jeremiah 5:23-24)

POETRY IN MOTION

SECONDLY, THE DESTINY PRINCIPLE PLAYS A SIGNIFICANT role in understanding the kairos point of miracles, and in increasing our awe of God.

Jeremiah 29:11 is another one of those verses I prefer in the KJV: "For I know the thoughts that I think toward you, saith the Lord, thoughts of peace, and not of evil, to give you an expected end."

I love that phrase "expected end." It implies God will finish the work He started in you and me. "...Being confident of this very thing, that He who has begun a good work in you will complete it until the day of Jesus Christ..." (Philippians 1:6) "He who calls you is faithful, who also will do it." (1 Thessalonians 5:24)

But when we take this principle in light of the "nowness" of God, we see that God has *already* finished your purpose, before you ever started it. Because it's all *just now* in the realm of God's eternality.

"Remember this, and show yourselves men; recall to mind, O you transgressors. Remember the former things of old, for I am God, and there is no other; I am God, and there is none like Me..." (Isaiah 46:8-9)

I think I've stated these concepts elsewhere, and they're not from me originally, but I wholeheartedly agree with these few statements: God creates the end from the beginning, then He ends. In other words, He starts at the end, and then He begins. He says, "I never begin something before I've ended it." So: just by the very fact you were born should tell you that God finished something for you to start. (Is your head spinning yet? *laugh*)

This is destiny. This is *now* kairos. Why are we pressing into the "awe" of God? Why are we going through the fires with the Lord and His Spirit? Because we have a purpose, an expected end, something God has already finished and it is our duty and mandate to start it for Him. Selah.

"For whom He foreknew, He also predestined to be conformed to the image of His Son, that He might be the firstborn among many brethren. Moreover whom He predestined, these He also called; whom He called, these He also justified; and whom He justified, these He also glorified." (Romans 8:29-30)

Called. Justified. Glorified. Things will happen. They just will. Why are you going to press into a greater intimacy with the Lord? Why are you going to subject yourself to the fires of testing? Why are you casting down so that you might perceive the "now-end" that God already ordained for you? Because you have no other choice... *grin* You've been called. You're saved, aren't you? You've been justified. You are glorified, at least as far as God perceives it (from the end, working in the now.) The process is happening *now*. You are destined.

Don't believe in destiny? Read John 9:1-9. Sorry. You're destined. Even the things you go through, the adversities and the fires, are to prove that God made you for a purpose. This is the *workmanship* of God principle.

I AM that I AM. That is His name. He *is*. And He is going to work in you what He destined for you at the end of the beginning, or the beginning of the end, or... well, you know what I mean. In His eternality and "presentness," He finished something that you will start.

"...To know the love of Christ which passes knowledge; that you may be filled with all the fullness of God." (Ephesians 3:19)

"And of His fullness we have all received, and grace for grace." (John 1:16)

Fullness. That's a great word. The Greek is *pleroma*. (Strong's #4138, "play-ROH-mah") and it speaks of how a ship is filled, or manned, with sailors, rowers and soldiers. It conveys a completeness, in the fullness of time, abundance and keeping full. It means "that which fills, or with which a thing is filled."

For our studies, we mean it as God's surplus, His over-abundance— the fullness which fills up the hollow places, as yet unfulfilled in our natures and characters. Literally, to be *crammed full*—a completion of a task or purpose. The fullness of God is poured within us so that the miracle we are seeking can be completed.

We have a destiny in God, where otherwise our lives would have no sense, no rhyme or reason, wherein we lived only for self-gratification, which is the opposite of fullness: disharmony, discord, and disarray. I have said elsewhere, and it bears repeating I think, that we are God's artistic expression set in motion. This is your purpose: to be God's poetry, His fine work of art, to be changed into a harmonious demonstration of God's beautiful craftsmanship.

"For we are His workmanship, created in Christ Jesus for good works, which God prepared beforehand that we should walk in them." (Ephesians 2:10)

Workmanship in the Greek is *poiema* (Strong's #4161, "poy-EH-mah") and by some clever bit of wordsmithing is where we have the English "poem." We're destined to be God's poem.

Recall 2 Corinthians 3:18 mentioned earlier. We are destined to be changed into the *same image*, glory to glory, by the Spirit. This is why increasing in the awe of God, developing reverential intimacy, going through the fires, is so important.

Thus should our prayer be: "The Lord will perfect that which concerns me; your mercy, O Lord, endures forever; do not forsake the works of Your hands." (Psalm 138:8)

Though your beginning may be small, He will perfect His workmanship in you, and though we start small and insignificant, at the end there is rapid acceleration. (Job 8:7)

We must define the "good works" of Ephesians 2:10 and *walk in them*. You were destined in a kairos moment to be God's poetry in motion, bringing the good works of the supernatural manifestation to a world that is dying to increase in the awe of God, whether they know it yet or not. This is the gold we purchase from our Lord and Lover, refined in fire. It is worth the cost!

So, the purpose of this book is to get you motivated to climb the mountain of glory so you, too, can be transfigured.

God as a Person

J ESUS SAID TO HER, 'WOMAN, BELIEVE ME, THE HOUR IS
coming when you will neither on this mountain, nor in Jerusalem,
worship the Father. You worship what you do not know; we know
what we worship, for salvation is of the Jews. But the hour is coming,
and now is, when the true worshipers will worship the Father in spirit
and truth; for the Father is seeking such to worship Him. God is Spirit,
and those who worship Him must worship in spirit and truth.'" (John
4:21-24)

Okay, go back to the Burning Bush experience of Exodus 3:1-15.
Moses asked a pretty critical question. "When I go to the children of
Israel, and I tell them the God of your fathers sent me, they're going to
ask me, 'Well, what's His name?' And what do I tell 'em?"

And God responds, "I AM WHO I AM."

One of the greatest revelation needs we have as children of God—
one of the main reasons why we don't communicate with Him as we
should, in an intimate lover-to-lover way, is because we fail to perceive
the Person of God. Yes, God is a Person. He is a spirit Being who has a
form and shape, albeit one that is completely, wholly changeless. And
though He is a consuming fire, He is also a Person, not a thing. Not a
mystical cosmic force, not a concept, not some "sky bully" as I've heard
some humanists refer to Him as.

When you get to heaven, I assure you, you will see a Person on the throne, your Father. Seated at His right hand in a glorified body will be His Son, your Lord. And you will also see a Spirit who is aptly named Holy Spirit. (In case you didn't know, I'm a Trinitarian. *smile* And if you have a notion to want to know why, read *Aletheia Eleutheroo.*) They are/is one sole, singular God, not three gods, eternally manifested as three distinct People.

We know that God is a Person, because the Bible says we are made in His image, in His form, only we are outwardly visibly on the earthly plane, whereas He (the Father) is a Spirit. And initially, we as a created race had an inward likeness (our inherent nature) to God as well, but we lost it when Adam and Eve fell into sin.

All right, enough basic Christian theology. Let's get to the point of this section. We know that I AM WHO I AM is an all-inclusive name that signifies three truths of the nature, the makeup, of God: HE IS omnipotent (all powerful), omniscient (all knowing) and omnipresent (all present.)

These are characteristics of God, who is All in All. Let's quickly identify some distinguishing elements of God's Person before we close this section. Shall we? Oh yes, please, let's shall.

God is all-speaking. He is the final authority on anything and everything, ever and always (that's all-inclusive across the board, in case you think I left a "but" out of there somewhere.) He has a voice. Psalm 29 talks about this voice, describing it as thunders. David describes His voice as one that breaks, divides, shakes and makes. He calls it powerful and full of majesty.

God is all-glory. He is the fullness of glory, power, majesty, weightiness, any of the dozen words we can use to describe "glory"—again, all-inclusively. He has a face. (Psalm 34:16)

God is all-seeing. If He has a face, of necessity He has eyes. (2

Chronicles 16:9) These eyes see all, outwardly and inwardly, nothing is hidden from His sight.

"And there is no creature hidden from His sight, but all things are naked and open to the eyes of Him to whom we must give account." (Hebrews 4:13)

Why, He even has eyelids.

"The Lord is in His holy temple, the Lord's throne is in heaven; His eyes behold, His eyelids test the sons of men." (Psalm 11:4)

God is all-hearing. If He has eyes, of necessity He has ears. In fact, He hears words in the minds of men. (Psalm 94:11) The Lord hears all, knows all and records all.

I've heard (heh-heh, that's clever) of the Lord giving that ability to His people sometimes, wherein they were able to hear the thoughts of people just as if they were speaking with their mouths. Not just in general—it wasn't some invasion of privacy—it was necessary for them to discern what was being thought at that particular time. And while I've never heard someone's thoughts as if they were speaking them aloud, I have had a gracious discernment of those thoughts, and that discernment has saved my life when others wished to do me bodily ill. So thank the Lord He always hears!

God is all-smelling. Yes, He has a nose that smells. (Isaiah 65:1-5) Malachi 1:11 speaks of incense being burned. God smells the sweet aroma of righteous worship, and sneezes the wicked right out!

God is all-powerful. He has very buff arms, and I'm not being facetious here. With His arm He heals, delivers and sets free. He restrains the works of the evil ones. He smashes the strongholds that bind His children. Indeed, God is a muscular Person.

"The Lord has made bare His holy arm in the eyes of all the nations; and all the ends of the earth shall see the salvation of our God... Who has believed our report? And to whom has the arm of the Lord been revealed?" (Isaiah 52:10; 53:1)

God is all-favorable and all-sustaining. The right hand of God speaks of favor and authority. This is where the Lord is seated, speaking of His exalted preeminence in all things, the ultimate favored place. (Check out Psalm 110:1; Matthew 25:31; Mark 16:19; Luke 22:69; John 17:5; Acts 2:33; 5:31; Romans 8:34; Ephesians 1:20; Colossians 3:1; Hebrews 1:3; 1:13; 8:1; 10:12; 12:2; 1 Peter 3:22; Revelation 3:21 for a few scriptural examples.)

"Behold, as the eyes of servants look to the hand of their masters, as the eyes of a maid to the hand of her mistress, so our eyes look to the Lord our God, until He has mercy on us." (Psalm 123:2)

God is all-sufficient in Himself. He is not lonely; He is God, clothed with shekinah glory.

"Bless the Lord, O my soul! O Lord my God, You are very great: You are clothed with honor and majesty, who cover Yourself with light as with a garment, who stretch out the heavens like a curtain." (Psalm 104:1-2)

What an amazing God we serve who gives His children a little taste of glory divine, those who are earnestly led of the Spirit, even through the fires of affliction, so that we might partake of even a touch of God's divine nature manifested through us.

"...But rejoice to the extent that you partake of Christ's sufferings, that when His glory is revealed, you may also be glad with exceeding joy... by which have been given to us exceedingly great and precious promises, that through these you may be partakers of the divine nature, having escaped the corruption that is in the world through lust." (1 Peter 4:13; 2 Peter 1:4)

God is all-sensitive. He possesses the same emotions that you do: He can be made angry; He can be jealous; He can be zealous; He desires, He loves, and He hates. He even feels sadness. It is a travesty to assume, if you are capable of a particular feeling, that God is unable to feel in an even greater measure than you (apart from an emotion leading to sin, of course.) Many well-meaning people, I suppose in an effort to appear reverential or overly pious perhaps, tend to depersonalize God, making Him into something that is incapable of feeling the same emotions that they are—because they imply that certain emotions are weakness. But it is not irreverent to attribute to God the emotions that He manifests Himself in the Bible, and it is only when emotions rule our lives that they become weaknesses.

God is all-timelessness. Our Creator is never bound in time. He dwells in eternity, past, present and future, simultaneously. He is infinite, and as such is not limited by space, time or matter.

"For thus says the High and Lofty One who inhabits eternity, whose name is Holy: 'I dwell in the high and holy place, with him who has a contrite and humble spirit, to revive the spirit of the humble, and to revive the heart of the contrite ones.'" (Isaiah 57:15)

In summation, God is all-complete. He covers the entire scope of human need, as revealed by His compound redemptive names. There is nothing we need apart from Him for utter fulfillment in anything. Period. We know this, but we must always keep this in the forefront of our thinking as we face the fires.

The Lord Jehovah's compound names are more fully expressed in my other writings, but let's highlight a couple of them here for the sake of being thorough concerning the Person of God.

HE IS our Peace (*Shalom*; Judges 6:24), brought nigh to us when the Father gave the Son to bridge the gap between God and man, once and for all. Jesus is the Father's ultimate testament that He wants peace between us. HE IS our Shepherd (*Raah*; Psalm 23:1), most perfectly manifested when our Lord gave His life for us. HE IS our Provider

(*Jireh*; Genesis 22:14), again most perfectly manifested when Jesus gave Himself as an offering for our salvation. HE IS our Banner (*Nissi*; Exodus 17:15)—our great Victor (Colossians 2:15)—overcoming every adversity and destroying every hindrance, providing direct access to the Father. HE IS our Righteousness (*Tsidkenu*; Jeremiah 23:6), when we receive the gift of Christ's atonement and glorification, we are made righteous (in right-standing) before the Father. HE IS our Physician (*Rapha*; Exodus 15:26), again emphasizing Christ's atoning work on the cross even for our physical infirmities. HE IS present in all things concerning us (*Shammah*; Ezekiel 48:35.)

He is never limited by a lack of strength (Habakkuk 3:19, as just one example—go Google some verses on God's strength), He never sleeps (Psalm 121:3-4), He never tires (Isaiah 40:28), and He never hungers (Psalm 50:12.) God cannot fail, cannot sin, and cannot lie. This is who you serve, this is who you go through the fires for, this is who we stand in awe of. Let Him be your fear. Behold your God! (Isaiah 40:9)—

"Then the earth shook and trembled; the foundations of the hills also quaked and were shaken because He was angry. Smoke went up from His nostrils, and devouring fire from His mouth; coals were kindled by it. He bowed the heavens also, and came down with darkness under His feet. And He rode upon a cherub, and flew; He flew upon the wings of the wind. He made darkness His secret place; His canopy around Him was dark waters and thick clouds of the skies. From the brightness before Him, His thick clouds passed with hailstones and coals of fire. The Lord thundered from heaven, and the Most High uttered His voice, hailstones and coals of fire. He sent out His arrows and scattered the foe, lightnings in abundance, and He vanquished them. Then the channels of the sea were seen, the foundations of the world were uncovered at Your rebuke, O Lord, at the blast of the breath of Your nostrils." (Psalm 18:7-15)

CRAVING GOD

ISAID JUST A LITTLE EARLIER THAT GOD DESIRES—AND more than anything about this creation of His, He desires *us*. (Only He knows why... *smile*) Nevertheless, He yearns for us, dare I say He is even covetous over us, as a husband is jealous over his own wife (or he *should* be, at any rate...) Desire, in and of itself, is not necessarily an evil force, though it can be corrupted. But in its purest state, we should be driven by our longing for the Lord, just as He is driven in His longing for us.

The need for "wanting" was initiated by God Himself when we were created. We were designed to need Him, to crave His attention, just as He longs for our unpolluted and freely-given worship and praise—because what else does one do with God but worship Him? That's the whole point of God to begin with—a Being worthy of worship, apart from anything He does or gives to us. It is not an alien, foreign concept to Him. He created us to need Him (whether fallen humanity wishes to acknowledge that or not) and He fashioned our world to ultimately be satisfied by Him.

My beautiful wife, Joy—who I am extremely jealous over, thank you very much!—is always quoting Psalm 145; it's one of her favorite passages.

"The eyes of all look expectantly to You, and You give them their food in due season. You open Your hand and satisfy the desire of every living thing." (Psalm 145:15-16)

This means that everything (*every living thing* is pretty much all inclusive, you know) finds its fulfillment in the Lord, even for their *food* according to Psalm 147. How much more so for humans and their need for acceptance and relationship with Almighty God?

In the midst of the fires of affliction, the testings and struggles that Christians face, we must increase in our awe of God, and likewise increase in our *craving* for Him. We must grow in our desire to want Him, to need Him, to hanker and pine for Him—"hanker" and "pine" are good Texas words, you have to say them with a southern drawl.

Man, Psalm 42 is one of the most beautiful, the imagery is astounding! It's called a contemplation. And it really is a good one, especially when we are in the midst of life's many distresses. I won't copy the whole song out, but you should put this book down and go memorize Psalm 42. Let me know when you're finished.

"As the deer pants for the water brooks, so pants my soul for You, O God. My soul thirsts for God, for the living God. When shall I come and appear before God? My tears have been my food day and night, while they continually say to me, 'Where is your God?'" (Psalm 42:1-3)

That "appear before God" is sometimes rendered, "When shall I see the face of God?"

This desire is instilled within people. It is placed there by Him—He originates the longing and fulfills the longing, in other words. Sadly, the effects of sin have corrupted these cravings into baser lusts as a mockery of the original desire. People convince themselves they have no need for God—they'll give some crummy excuse like, "How can God be good when His creation is suffering so badly?" As if that lets them off the hook for the gnawing emptiness within them. But like the Bible notes, were it not for God's pressing, chasing, ravenous kindheartedness, "there is none who does good, no, not one." (Psalm 14:3)

Pretty sad testament. But see, the world does not have an *awe* of

God. They're not impressed as they should be. And what a dangerous position to be in... They have turned Him into a "thing" (if they acknowledge Him at all) instead of a Person who has wants and desires of His own—that is, a relationship with His creation. And so *the one* Person who can fulfill anything they lack, they ignore to their own detriment and peril—completing the cycle of why "bad things" happen in a good world. Of course, God gets all the blame, but they never give Him the love He is seeking.

And it's not just the world. Christians do this too, sometimes unwittingly from a veiled understanding of God as a Person, sometimes wantonly from an un-surrendered part of their lives. Yet, praise God for His grace, that desire is still chasing them, pursuing them, in some cases *tackling* them until God has their undivided attention. These are the fires. The things that God permits us to go through, to burn away the "ho-hum" attitude toward Him, until we turn to Him completely and say, "Okay, You have my attention." And then we perceive He was exactly what was lacking all along, and we're left with an ever-increasing awe-ness (I made that word up.)

"Where have You been all my life?" Stupid question, but thankfully one that can be put to rest once we are truly intimate with the Lord.

We owe it to the world to bring that awe-ness to them. Sure, there'll still be some thick-headed people out there. God only knows what it would take to break through those shells! But for the vast majority of the world, they'd just be happy to know that God *wants* them very badly.

But God won't spoon-feed people. There has to be a response on all our parts, Christian or otherwise. While He creates the longing, and is ultimately the One who fulfills that longing, there must be a willful act on behalf of the person to seek Him. (Psalm 27:8)

"But without faith it is impossible to please Him, for he who comes

51

to God must believe that He is, and that He is a rewarder of those who diligently seek Him." (Hebrews 11:6)

The fact of the matter is we must submit to the Lord for that desire to be satisfied. God isn't interested in slaves and servants, He's interested in obedient children—those who are in His family, with a place of authority and honor, and yet those who know from whence their bread is buttered, if you catch my meaning. Submission is not a robotic act of surrendering, something done grudgingly because one is at the end of a swordpoint, but rather it is an act of joyous yielding to One who is wiser, stronger, and more capable of meeting our desires.

This is why Christ is King—a good king is one beloved of his people, benevolent and merciful, possessing the qualities necessary to better the lifestyles of his subjects. God is not a tyrant, and any religion that says otherwise is either uneducated or polluted in its own mire as a form of control over its constituents.

We all know that the very definition of God is a Being who can *force* His will on anyone or anything. Otherwise, this Being wouldn't be God, right? But only a good God, while recognizing He *could* do so, would *not* do so. Even if that means leaving people to make dumb decisions that cause the "bad things" in life they blame on Him.

There is a difference between coming to Him and submitting willingly, and being forced to one's knees 'cause He's gonna blast you to smithereens.

And yet, the Lord *does* allow the fires to bring us to a place where we understand that by yielding to Him, our cravings are fulfilled. Again, there is a proper fear of the Lord that is an exercise of wisdom, not a response to terror.

But no matter what, God is not in the business of coercion—He's not the Godfather. Never forget God is love. Not He *has* love, He *is* love. And we know perfect love casts out fear. (1 John 4:18) As we encounter more awe-ness in the love of the Father, we voluntarily decide to surrender more and more to Him, and the fires are less and less.

The people who have not come to Him, almost without exception, have a veiled understanding of God's love. They view Him as a taskmaster up in the skies somewhere with lightning bolts aimed at them. They do not understand that His wrath (if He has love, He must have wrath; otherwise He is not a Person, but only half a One) is an extension of His awesome holiness—He cannot compromise one aspect of His Person for another.

It's always odd to me to see people expect God to be nothing but sweet and merciful, almost like some sort of cosmic butler, to do this or that for them—and yet, they can't seem to reconcile the fact that if *they* have a sense of justice, that God also would have a sense of justice, even more so being perfectly holy. If God is capable of infinite grace and love, He is capable of infinite righteous anger. Why is it humanity is allowed to understand right and wrong, and that there are consequences to one's actions—but God is not? Only they get to choose what is "fair" and "right"—but apparently God only has one way He can be.

"Now do not be stiff-necked, as your fathers were, but yield yourselves to the Lord; and enter His sanctuary, which He has sanctified forever, and serve the Lord your God, that the fierceness of His wrath may turn away from you." (2 Chronicles 30:8)

What this is *not* saying is, "God hates you and wants to make you miserable." What this *is* saying is: "Don't be a dolt, you can enter His sanctuary if you yield, and His wrath will be turned away."

Yielding is different than surrendering. In medieval times, let's say two knights were battling one-on-one. If one knight knocked his opponent down, the fallen knight could *yield* and he would then be protected by the greater knight. This was not seen as cowardice, it was not a loss of honor, it was seen as prudent. Only an arrogant (stiff-necked) knight wouldn't yield. And then that arrogant knight would be *forced* to surrender, forfeiting all he had, even to the point of losing his life. Yielding is different than surrendering, see.

The yielded knight was treated with courtesy and respect, and in fact, so long as his actions were not treasonous, a good king would restore him to his rightful lands and titles once the war was over.

That's not to say everyone in medieval times was chivalrous, I'm not naïve; but I just use it as an illustration to point out that submitting to God is not the same as selling yourself to God at swordpoint. And if medieval lords could be gracious, how much more so God, who is love?

We as a race need to have an awe-encounter with God above, wherein we come to a greater understanding of God's infinite love and God's infinite holiness. No one can claim God is unjust. If He had not provided the means for us to approach Him through His Son, then yes, it would be unfair, because many of us would *want* to yield to Him and would be unable to do so. Yet the fact remains, Jesus is available to each and every person drawing breath on this planet, no matter what they've done... or what they think of Him. All we have to do is yield.

And one last thought on this before we move on: it's my experience and understanding as I study scripture that giving oneself willingly to the Lord is a process of a lifetime. It's unrealistic to assume that a person, when he or she comes to the Lord, can relinquish *every* facet of their life all in one swoop. Would be nice and easy, just doesn't work that way. It's also unrealistic to say, "I give it *all* to You, Jesus. You have it all." While the motive may be correct, bottom line is "all" is simply another way of remaining *vague*. So what happens is *nothing* in particular is given to Him, just "all"—does that make sense?

The work of the Holy Spirit, and indeed the fires of testing, is to bring specific things out into the open between you and God. The good news is, you don't have to be perfected to be worthwhile. And while some of you may think you're just a total mess and how is God *ever* going to get to the bottom of everything you need to yield—you are a finite person. There's only so much of you to go around. God knows what He's doing—it's up to us to give those things to Him as He points them out. If God is truly good, then whatever He asks of you is for your own good.

Here and There

ONE LAST COMPONENT TO GOD'S PERSON BEFORE WE close this section down: I have spent many, many pages in other works discussing the "otherness" of God—His complete transcendence over all things—He is high and lifted up. (Isaiah 6:1) He is wholly separate and apart, and the only means we have of approaching Him is on His terms, through His Son.

The reason I have spent so much time devoted to God's transcendence is because I believe it is one of the vital keys that is often missing in Christians' walks. They don't see the breakthroughs they are looking for because they are lacking transcendent encounters in Him, where they come up higher into His presence and glory. There they are transfigured and changed, and what they are seeking is found at His throne.

"God is greatly to be feared in the assembly of the saints, and to be held in reverence by all those around Him." (Psalm 89:7)

There is a reason God is to be feared and revered. This is His transcendent position above everything else. Words that were used to describe Him by our predecessors were "awful" and "terrible." These words connote something different nowadays, but the original meanings are accurate. God is "full of awe," and the thrust of this book is to highlight the necessity for increasing in that awe. You may or may not be aware that the Greek word for "holy" (Strong's #40, *hagios,* "hag-EE-oss") means "other" or rather, "different from everything else." It can be rendered "terrible" in the archaic sense of the word—not "this tastes terrible" but rather "God is terribly mighty."

We must be made aware of this "other" aspect of God's Person, it doesn't receive as much emphasis in the body of Christ as it should. And yet, there is another facet to God: His nearness, or His immanence. Closeness. Right here-ness.

And if you stop to think about it, both of those facets are just as "awe-full" as the other. As we enter into Spirit-led transcendent encounters, we cannot "decrease" the importance of God's personal imminence and contact. Otherwise, we run the risk of depersonalizing Him into something so "other" we can't hope to grasp what He's about.

The purpose of the fires of testing is, therefore, two-fold: to increase our awe of God's transcendence, but also to draw us closer to Him in an immanent relationship. There must be a balance between the "glory encounters" and the "lovemaking" with God. If we focus too heavily on getting up there with Him, we can miss out on being with Him here. Conversely, if we focus too heavily on being near to Him, we can become almost lackadaisical, or complacently casual, about the transcendence of God. The "other" encounters with God's glory should in turn increase our awe at His nearness. We're small, He's infinitely large, and yet, He wants to be right here, with us, right now.

You're probably aware of the Hebrew word *yada* (Strong's 3045, "YAH-dah") and it's a verb meaning "to know." Interesting to note that yada can imply a progression of "coming to know" someone as a process, seeking out, finding and perceiving. To learn about someone, to get to know someone by experience.

So, this means we must yada God to understand His hagios-ness. It is a close-encounter yada experience that reveals His otherness, and vice versa. Both facets of His Person must be incorporated in our relationship with Him to increase in our awe of Him.

Luckily for us, God *wants* to reveal His glory (Habakkuk 3:3-4), albeit to a worthy audience. He doesn't just throw it around recklessly— it is something He guards very carefully, because He is hagios. And yet, He desires intimacy with us, so much so, that He bridged the gap between His transcendence and His immanence through Jesus Christ.

"For it is the God who commanded light to shine out of darkness, who has shone in our hearts to give the light of the knowledge of the glory of God in the face of Jesus Christ." (2 Corinthians 4:6)

It is my desire in the confines of this book to help in a small way to increase your understanding of God's Person, and thus increase in your awe of Him. So let's continue on, shall we?

CELEBRATING LIFE

IN ITS SIMPLEST DEFINITION, THE FEAR OF THE LORD IS A hatred toward anything that is contrary to His ways. You fear Him because He is holy, and that righteous fear drives you to holiness. Not fear of reprisal, but rather fear of doing that which takes God's presence away from you, that which is sin. (Psalm 51:11)

"The fear of the Lord is to hate evil; pride and arrogance and the evil way and the perverse mouth I hate." (Proverbs 8:13)

If the wages of sin is death (Romans 6:23), then the fear of the Lord is the reward of life—since it directly opposes sin. God abhors sin, it is contradictory to His Person. Therefore, the means by which we can keep God's commandment to be holy (Leviticus 19:2) is through an intimate relationship with Jesus. Since He is holy, the closer we are to Him, the more His holiness shines through us—His holiness shining through us is the manifestation of the sons of God (Romans 8:19; sons are disciplined ones, see? The word *disciple* means "to show forth one's discipline"), which in turn yields the miraculous we are seeking.

The signs, wonders and miracles are a direct by-product of holiness unto the Lord through intimacy with Him. The fires of testing is the means by which the Holy Spirit teaches us to yield to His holiness. If God is just (2 Thessalonians 1:6; Psalm 25:8), then it is against His Person to set forth a standard that is impossible for us to hold to. All that means is you can do all things through Christ (Philippians 4:13), even being holy. Can you do it in your own strength? Of course not. But in an intimate relationship with Christ, you *can* be holy.

"My covenant was with him, one of life and peace, and I gave them to him that he might fear Me; so he feared Me and was reverent before My name." (Malachi 2:5)

A covenant of life and peace, given so that we might fear Him—without an understanding of the fear of the Lord, that sounds contrary. Life, peace, fear. I once heard from an atheist who was using Abraham's sacrificing Isaac as "proof" of the "absurdity" of the existence of God—how could a loving God demand a father to offer up his son; it's just barbaric and irrational. (Never mind the fact that God *spared* Isaac... but hey, I've never claimed atheism was the height of rational intelligence...) Sadly, this stems from a veiled understanding of God as a Person.

We recognize Abraham offering Isaac as a foreshadowing of God who offered His own Son, but of course, atheists say that's irrational and stupid, too. I'm not trying to convince atheists here, I just want to point out God's response to Abraham:

"And He said, 'Do not lay your hand on the lad, or do anything to him; for now I know that you fear God, since you have not withheld your son, your only son, from Me.'" (Genesis 22:12)

This was a fire of testing for Abraham. And the result was God's acknowledgement of Abraham's fear, resulting in Isaac's life. God moreover proved His "fear of Himself" (if I can phrase it that way; that is, He proved His holiness) by not withholding His Son, His only Son, from us. Thus establishing a perpetual covenant of life and peace (Hebrews 8:6) for those who believe in God's fear (His holiness) by yielding to His Son, who was resurrected from death. (Romans 8:11)

And so, how do you know you fear the Lord? You want to obey Him. You show forth your discipline. If you do, you are a friend of God.

(John 15:14-17) It is always better to be a friend of God than an enemy. Just makes sense, right?

This is why Proverbs 23:17 says, "Do not let your heart envy sinners, but be zealous for the fear of the Lord all the day..."

What we're talking about here is the law of the Spirit of life in Christ Jesus which frees us from the law of sin and death. (Romans 8:2) This is the subject of Peter's powerful proclamation (that's alliterative...) in Acts 2, specifically versus 22-36, if you would like to read them.

It is a proclamation of a celebration (more alliteration...)—a celebration of the resurrection of Jesus, a celebration of life, a celebration of approval, a celebration of acceptance (as in Luke 4:19, "the acceptable year of the Lord," a time of Jubilee.) The resurrection is not just a story to be told—it's to be experienced.

So what does it mean to celebrate life? "...I have come that they may have life, and that they may have it more abundantly." (John 10:10) Life abundantly means to experience a richness and quality above measure, literally "to throw beyond." First it stretches you, then it propels you into a state of completeness, beyond ordinary measure. It implies being made whole. The experience of the resurrection celebrates a life beyond the minimal, a life of comprehensive fullness in all facets. That's something to celebrate, huh?

When Christ was "lifed" into resurrection, it set the stage for the Spirit to proclaim a celebration of abundance, and note that in Acts 2:22, that word "attested"—it means approval as in, "...God also bearing witness both with signs and wonders, with various miracles, and gifts of the Holy Spirit, according to His own will..." (Hebrews 2:4) It is a stamp of God's approval, initiated by the life-ing of Christ, a life so abundant in excess, that once we have accepted it, there is more than enough to give away to others. We can be used to be an abundant blessing to others.

This celebration of life is to be so great in you that it creates a celebration in the lives of others. We are to be walking in the light of His life. This is why, "Every good gift and every perfect gift is from above, and comes down from the Father of lights, with whom there is no variation or shadow of turning." (James 1:17)

God wants to place His approval on you, a member of the corporate Body. We can define approval as "exhibiting greatness." It means to prove the worth of the resurrection by demonstration, and it's cyclical: in the demonstrating, it brings about the approval. Sadly, it is a lack of intimacy with Him as a Person, a lack of holy fear, too, that keeps many measures of life-ing from being experienced.

Those "divers miracles" from Hebrews 2:4 (KJV) are the many manifestations that bring about the proof of the approval under the law of the Spirit of life. They are the celebration of the many-colored, many-faceted expression of God. The Father of lights, indeed!

LIVING A LIFE OF LIGHT

CHRIST LIVED (AND LIVES) A LIFE OF LIGHT. HE HAD AN understanding of the fear of the Lord and was approved and honored by the Father, given the Spirit without measure.

"The Spirit of the Lord shall rest upon Him, the Spirit of wisdom and understanding, the Spirit of counsel and might, the Spirit of knowledge and of the fear of the Lord. His delight is in the fear of the Lord, and He shall not judge by the sight of His eyes, nor decide by the hearing of His ears..." (Isaiah 11:2-3)

If it was vital for the Lord to understand this, it must equally be important for us to increase in the awe of God, to develop our understanding of proper fear, so that we might be a demonstration and a celebration of that abundant life to all the world.

"Let all the earth fear the Lord; let all the inhabitants of the world stand in awe of Him. For He spoke, and it was done; He commanded, and it stood fast." (Psalm 33:8-9)

This celebratory life of light, tempered by the Lord in the fires, is to be a demonstration of God's greatness to the world. It gives validity to the claim of Jesus' victorious triumph over the enemies of death, hell and the grave.

"...Whom God raised up, having loosed the pains of death, because it was not possible that He should be held by it." (Acts 2:24)

Loosed the pains of death to be a testament of light to the world.

This is what we celebrate in the resurrection. God the Father gave witness (His approval) to His Son by raising Him from the dead. This is why Acts 4:33 shows, "And with great power the apostles gave witness to the resurrection of the Lord Jesus. And great grace was upon them all." Approval/witness. This is the resting of God's honor—His reputation, His worth—on His people, placed upon them through the resurrection of the Son.

But it is the *expression* of the Lord's honor that gives other people a good opinion of God. I've said elsewhere that the word glory (Strong's #1391, *doxa*, "DOX-uh") means an opinion of someone's worth. Referring to Christ, it is His "most exalted state"—His "most glorious condition"—upon being raised from the dead. The expression of that glorified state of the Son, the demonstration of victory in your lives, is what brings glory to God. This is why we celebrate.

"Therefore we were buried with Him through baptism into death, that just as Christ was raised from the dead by the glory of the Father, even so we also should walk in newness of life." (Romans 6:4)

The reason we press through the fires of testing, why we develop an ever-increasing awe of God, is because we have an acute understanding that He wants to give witness of His Son *through His people*. We are to be witnesses of the resurrection and glorification of Christ.

"This Jesus God has raised up, of which we are all witnesses." (Acts 2:32)

And you're probably aware that "witness" in the Greek is *martys* (Strong's #3144, "MAR-toos"), wherein we get the word *martyr*. In its strictest sense, it means a witness in a legal proceeding, one giving testimony (assuming a truthful portrayal of the facts.) According to Thayer's, it most likely stems from a word meaning "one who is mindful," one who pays attention, akin to the Latin word *memor*, which you'll recognize as "memory." From a Christian standpoint the word is used for one who follows in Christ's example by testifying of their faith, even and especially to the point of death.

"If we receive the witness of men, the witness of God is greater; for this is the witness of God which He has testified of His Son." (1 John 5:10)

It means one who bears witness (that's deep)—"one whose life and actions testify to the worth and effect of their faith, and whose faith in turn receives witness in Scripture." Celebrating the spiritual life of Christ even to the point of physical death.

God witnesses of our witness by backing up our faith with results according to Scripture. While being a physical martyr may be the ultimate testing by fire, it is still applicable in a spiritual sense, that we testify of God's truth in His Son, and in return that truth is testified by a demonstration of His Son's power over death, sicknesses, etc.

"The elders who are among you I exhort, I who am a fellow elder and a witness of the sufferings of Christ, and also a partaker of the glory that will be revealed..." (1 Peter 1:5)

We should be witnesses of great power and great grace! One of the primary reasons we should increase in our awe of God, submit ourselves to the fires of testing, is so that we might be a witness to the resurrection, to celebrate life. And what is life? Or rather, how do we give witness to that life we're speaking of?

The life we're speaking of, of course, is the life of Christ Jesus, for, "In Him was life, and the life was the light of men." (John 1:4) This life of Christ's *inspires* us, it *increases* us, and gives us *intelligence*—(three I's, that's homiletics)—it gives an understanding of the Father and His ways. It gives in over-abundance, enthusing us to ever-increasing heights of demonstrating this life to others. We must learn to walk in the light of this life; we must press into this life in an even deeper way than what we have experienced in the past. This life cannot stagnate, but rather must grow and grow as we become greater witnesses of this life.

Like Peter quotes Psalm 16, "'You have made known to me the ways of life; you will make me full of joy in Your presence.'" (Acts 2:28) We, too, must be made to know the ways of life. The point of the fires is *not* to make us miserable. On the contrary, it is to dazzle us with the glory and majesty of Christ the King so as to forge within us an expression of His life to others. Just as He died and rose again, in Him, we must die and be raised in the newness of life, receiving of His glorification so that we might present it to others.

"That which was from the beginning, which we have heard, which we have seen with our eyes, which we have looked upon, and our hands have handled, concerning the Word of life—the life was manifested, and we have seen, and bear witness, and declare to you that eternal life which was with the Father and was manifested to us..." (1 John 1:1-2)

The ways of life. So when it says, "In Him was life," because of the resurrection, we give witness to Christ as the foundation of life. He is the expression of life. He is the law of life. Our faith is not in vain, dear readers! (See 1 Corinthians 15.) Again, Peter quotes David: "'Therefore my heart rejoiced, and my tongue was glad; moreover my flesh also will rest in hope.'" (Acts 2:26) We, too, have the rest in hope of Christ's glorious resurrection—this is why we celebrate life!

And I'm sure you know "life" in the Greek is *zoe* (Strong's #2222, "ZOH-eh.") The law of zoe (back to Romans 8:2, if you've forgotten) is a present, absolute word, meaning complete and in the now. It stems from a root meaning to enjoy a real life, a true life worthy of the name "life" in all its many facets. Active and blessed, full of vigor, strong, powerful, efficient and efficacious.

Strong's defines it as: "of the absolute fulness of life, both essential and ethical, which belongs to God, and through him both to the hypostatic 'logos' and to Christ in whom the 'logos' put on human nature; life real and genuine, a life active and vigorous, devoted to God, blessed, in the portion even in this world of those who put their trust in Christ, but after the resurrection to be consummated by new accessions (among them a more perfect body), and to last for ever."

However you want to phrase it, it means exceedingly full of life in abundance. So, in Him, was *this* kind of life—the light of men. It is life as God has it, the expression of life in its highest, most complete and perfected form. Life in the most extreme quantity and life in the most extreme quality. And this is the life we possess in Christ! This is why we celebrate.

"For as the Father has life in Himself, so He has granted the Son to have life in Himself..." (John 5:26) "In this the love of God was manifested toward us, that God has sent His only begotten Son into the world, that we might live through Him." (1 John 4:9)

It's not an exact quote, but John Lake defined the law of life as: by the action of one's will, a person can purposely put themselves in contact with God. Faith takes possession of his heart, and the condition of his nature is changed. Instead of being fearful, he is faith-filled. Instead of being absorbent and drawing everything to himself that is negative and destructive, his spirit repels sickness and disease—the Spirit of Christ's resurrection power flows through the whole being and emanates through the hands, heart, and from every pore of the body. When men turn their faces heavenward and look to Jesus for salvation, instantly by faith they contact the law of life—Jesus is the law of life— life comes from His soul; He breathes it into our hearts; He plants it into our natures; He transmits it into our bodies—that is what makes people whole!

Something to that extent.

Look, we need a quickening. The point of increasing in the awe of God is to create a celebratory expression and demonstration of Christ's resurrection to those outside of the Body (well, and many within!) One of the primary purposes of walking with the Lord in the fires—yes, even the glorified sufferings in Christ—is to draw us in faith toward the life of Christ. And while celebration and suffering seem contradictory, it is from an unveiled understanding of the law of life that we are drawn into an even greater stance of wonderment and reverence toward the Father, in whom is life and life in all its over-abundance.

What we're talking about here is the miracle of the newness of life, a life that restores, a life that imparts continually the actual life of Jesus within us.

We need a quickening of the Spirit for, "It is the Spirit who gives life; the flesh profits nothing. The words that I speak to you are spirit, and they are life." (John 6:63) "But if the Spirit of Him who raised Jesus from the dead dwells in you, He who raised Christ from the dead will also give life to your mortal bodies through His Spirit who dwells in you." (Romans 8:11)

And this was Peter's point in Acts 2, "Therefore being exalted to the right hand of God, and having received from the Father the promise of the Holy Spirit, He poured out this which you now see and hear." (Verse 33)

Indeed, the true message of the resurrection is at the heart of Pentecost! Amen. This is why we celebrate life!

STRONGHAND

REMEMBER ISAIAH 8, "FOR THE LORD SPOKE THUS TO ME with a strong hand..." (Verse 11) There's a concept here I'd like to look into for a bit: the might of His hand. It flows well with our understanding of the Person of God, to look at His "muscularity" if I can phrase it that way.

I believe in the ministry of laying on of hands, but perhaps I can add another facet to it that ties into our theme of increasing in the awe of God. I think we as the Body need to have a new infusion of understanding of what is released and what is imparted when we lay hands on others. I want to discuss a few points that might assist us in this kind of dimension release of power that results in the awe-encounters we're talking about in this book.

The miraculous power of Jesus flowing through our hands as empty vessels creates an astonishment, a reverence, even a sense of holy fear.

"So great fear came upon all the church and upon all who heard these things. And through the hands of the apostles many signs and wonders were done among the people. And they were all with one accord in Solomon's Porch. Yet none of the rest dared join them, but the people esteemed them highly. And believers were increasingly added to the Lord, multitudes of both men and women, so that they brought the sick out into the streets and laid them on beds and couches, that at least the shadow of Peter passing by might fall on some of them. Also a multitude gathered from the surrounding cities to Jerusalem, bringing sick people and those who were tormented by unclean spirits, and they were all healed." (Acts 5:11-16)

I've discussed in other books the "unusual" miracles wrought by Paul (Acts 19:11-12), and for the purpose of our book here, we'll just restate that these were *extraordinary* miracles, which is kind of humorous because does that mean there are "ordinary" miracles? Well, from a certain viewpoint, yes.

In this instance, we are talking about an encounter that stretched beyond the "ordinary" encounters with God. Something was expressed and revealed beyond the actual miracles themselves. Under the apostles hands, the people were *marked* with the imprint of God Himself. It changed them, they were permanently altered in a way they had never experienced before. I believe we are to be a people chosen by God to express this kind of marked extraordinariness—I believe there is a remnant, a group of watchmen and watchwomen (see Revelation 7 and Ezekiel 3—and note that Ezekiel was "astonished.")

The finger of God is heavy, as Isaiah would attest. That "heavy hand" phrase connotes a weight and a burden placed upon the prophet—the desires and zeal of God literally weighed Isaiah down. The Lord gave him a strong impression of power and a strong impression of purpose—indeed, the very imprint of His Person upon His mouthpiece.

It is the same for special miracles. When someone receives an extraordinary experience with the Person of God, he or she comes to an astonished understanding that God does not *just* heal—He *is* healing. An aspect of His Person is revealed to them, beyond just the physical infirmity or mental anguish being healed. They are given a living piece of evidence that God is very much real, and very much powerful. His might and power are made alive to them, and the imprint of His Person can be felt, seen and heard. The Word is made flesh. (John 1:14)

Just as Psalm 107:20 says "He sent His word and healed them, and delivered them from their destruction," we're talking about a vocal, tangible, heavy touch from Almighty God. It is this brush with His might that enables us to withstand any attack, to successfully oppose the enemy that wars against us.

Note the "full armor" section of Ephesians 6: "Finally, my brethren, be strong in the Lord and in the power of His might." (Verse 10) The Greek word for "be strong" is *endynamoo* (Strong's #1743, "EN-do-NA-mo-oh") meaning, "a power whose purpose is to infuse a believer with an excessive dose of inward strength." It conveys the thought of an explosive power (the root is *dynamis*, where we get "dynamite" appropriately enough) that is deposited into some type of specially prepared container, vessel or receptacle (that's you...)

The word "power" is *kratos* (Strong's #2904, "KRAY-tos"), and it is an eruptive, explosive, tangible demonstration of dominion—it is an external, outward manifestation of demonstrated power that can be seen, heard and felt. A mighty deed. It is *real* power.

"...And what is the exceeding greatness of His power toward us who believe, according to the working of His mighty power which He worked in Christ when He raised Him from the dead and seated Him at His right hand in the heavenly places..." (Ephesians 1:19-20)

That kind of power. The kind of power that raised Jesus from the dead—with His glory upon us, we have that kind of resurrection power working in us to create an awe-encounter with the Father, the kind that changes people permanently. The strongest kind of power known to God and man! It is available. We have to forge an expectation to see this kind of power manifested, for it seeks an avenue of release to demonstrate itself, to make God known and real to the world, and it is for this that we are with the Lord in the fires. To make ourselves available and ready to receive that "heavy hand."

God is able, mighty; He's muscular! The Greek word for "might" is *ischys* (Strong's #2479, "EE-skuse," sort of...) and it speaks of ability in strength, connoting a mighty man with great muscular capabilities, a strongman, a man with strong hands. It is derived from a word conveying having or holding something in one's hands, the ability to lay hold of something, the ability to possess, literally "to have." It means to be buff.

So *kratos* is the outwardly demonstrated power, erupting, manifesting from the hands of God, and *ischys* is the force, the ability, that works behind the *kratos*.

Why is *kratos* so strong and demonstrative? That resurrection power working through our hands to create extraordinary miracles? Because God's muscles are backing it up!

His Person. We're talking about a revelation of His strength and might that increases our awe of Him. All that He is, all the energy He possesses, being made manifest to us. This is how we can be strong in the Lord, and the powerful, outwardly demonstrated ability working in us is given as a result of God's great muscular ability in those strong hands working behind the scenes.

This is how John can say, "You are of God, little children, and have overcome them, because He who is in you is greater than he who is in the world." (1 John 4:4) He knew this from a first hand experience. Like him, you are a specially created receptacle, uniquely made to express the power of God's might. So be strong! Be endynamoo! In-dynamited.

See, there must be a receiver for this power to be deposited into. We have been especially designed by God to be the receptacles of His divine power. This goes back to the *poiema* from earlier.

When you have an understanding that you were *created* to be infused with a supernatural strength and ability, backed by God's strong hands—you were fashioned to be a special container of this phenomenal power built upon God's muscular Person—it should create an overwhelming "awe" moment in your life, a seeing beyond the norm, envisioning the bigger picture of *why* the fires of testing are so important. This receptacle of God's *kratos* is fashioned by fire, tested and refined, hardened by flames, so to speak. This is the gold we're buying from Jesus (again, Revelation 3:18.)

He is asking us, "Will you be empowered with this special, heavy touch of God's strength? It's costly, it weighs a lot—God's glory is hefty." But see, He knows it's cyclical: the fires create the container for this inner-strengthening, which uphold us in the fires.

But we war against a spirit of stupor. A blindness, a deafness, a glazing of indifference that is the dross in the fires. It tries to place a hood over our eyes, its weak, pestilential hands around our ears, whispering, "You don't want to experience the muscularity of God! Be weak, be passively content to sit in the dark, seeing nothing, hearing nothing, doing nothing. Just take a nap. Better than the fires..."

You don't believe it's a real spirit out there?

"Yet the Lord has not given you a heart to perceive and eyes to see and ears to hear, to this very day." (Deuteronomy 29:4)

"Pause and wonder! Blind yourselves and be blind! They are drunk, but not with wine; they stagger, but not with intoxicating drink. For the Lord has poured out on you the spirit of deep sleep, and has closed your eyes, namely, the prophets; and He has covered your heads, namely, the seers. The whole vision has become to you like the words of a book that is sealed, which men deliver to one who is literate, saying, 'Read this, please.' And he says, 'I cannot, for it is sealed.'" (Isaiah 29:9-11)

"Just as it is written: 'God has given them a spirit of stupor, eyes that they should not see and ears that they should not hear, to this very day.'" (Romans 11:8)

Don't go to sleep, don't stumble around in a blind, deaf, dark stupor.

Open your eyes, open your ears! You were made to increase in the awe of God! Might be a little silly, but oh-so-appropriate; you remember that Power Team T-shirt from the '80s? "God made you to <u>win</u>!" (You have to underline <u>win</u>.)

Okay, I'll stop. Look, this is serious. One of the primary reasons for the anointing is to break those yokes of bondage. (Isaiah 10:27) To throw off that hood, to open those ears. To muzzle that spirit of stupor and sleep. The enemy would like nothing better than to enslave us to sickness, disease, death, complacency—even religion! But thankfully the weapons of our warfare are not carnal. (2 Corinthians 10:4) We have the anointing to break these yokes, and so apropos of God's muscularity, we would do well to talk about that anointing for a little bit. Shall we?

Anointing and Leaven

IN AND OF OURSELVES, WE CANNOT CAST OFF THE SPIRIT of stupor. Without God's muscular assistance, through the help of the Holy Spirit, we cannot fully overcome. It takes an "excellent spirit" (Daniel 5:12) to be able to untie the knots of the spirit of stupor. It takes the anointing. Thankfully, the Spirit is not stingy with that anointing!

"But you have an anointing from the Holy One, and you know all things... Therefore let that abide in you which you heard from the beginning. If what you heard from the beginning abides in you, you also will abide in the Son and in the Father. And this is the promise that He has promised us—eternal life. These things I have written to you concerning those who try to deceive you. But the anointing which you have received from Him abides in you, and you do not need that anyone teach you; but as the same anointing teaches you concerning all things, and is true, and is not a lie, and just as it has taught you, you will abide in Him. And now, little children, abide in Him, that when He appears, we may have confidence and not be ashamed before Him at His coming." (1 John 2:20, 24-28)

What an awesome passage, what a great assurance! The anointing is to abide within us.

You most likely know that "Christ" is a title (not a surname, *grin*) and it means "Anointed." Strong's #5547 is *Christos* ("KREE-stoss"), used almost six hundred times in the New Testament, referring to Jesus as the Anointed Son of God. It stems from the root *chrio* (Strong's #5548, "KREE-oh") meaning "to be touched by the hand," to be "smeared."

The verb form (see Strong's #5530) implies receiving something on loan, borrowing something and taking it for one's own, to make use of it for one's benefit. To handle.

And it figuratively speaks of God's might and power (see Strong's #5495)—*the same activity and agency God exercised in creating the universe*—lent to another to protect, aid, uphold and preserve that person.

The point is, the anointing is something to be experienced. Because Jesus is entitled "the Christ," it's a term that is supposed to point toward something we are to encounter—it is an event, a happening, an occurrence. A brush with the anointing.

And you might be shocked to read this, but even our Lord Jesus, whilst on this earth, was utterly reliant upon that anointing as well. It wasn't enough for the Father to just name Jesus "the Christ"—the Son Himself had to encounter that anointing and take it for His own in order to accomplish what the Father wanted done on the earth.

Yes, Jesus was fully God. And He was fully Man; thus He had to be enabled by an experience with the Father's anointing in order to live beyond those human restrictions—to act supernaturally on the Father's behalf. Jesus is our great Example, and therefore, we too must be anointed. This is why Christian mean "little anointed one."

It was the anointing that empowered and facilitated the Christ to do what He saw the Father doing, to say only what He heard the Father say. Jesus revealed the Father's heavenly realm to the earth through the use of the anointing.

"...How God anointed Jesus of Nazareth with the Holy Spirit and with power, who went about doing good and healing all who were oppressed by the devil, for God was with Him." (Acts 10:38)

After the Temptation in the wilderness, we see that the Lord returned in the power of the Spirit (Luke 4:14) and proclaimed, "...'The time is fulfilled, and the kingdom of God is at hand. Repent, and believe in the gospel.'" (Mark 1:15)

It is the anointing that brought the kingdom of God to hand. The anointing showed by demonstration and experience that the kingdom of God was here, now, a reality of present time—not just some future hope of destination.

This is why I am convinced the miraculous brings an experience of the anointing to the people—it sets in motion something we can receive and inherit for ourselves. The anointing, through the miraculous, breeds the anointing. The anointing creates an avenue for the supernatural to move through, establishing an experience for mankind that is to become part of their daily existence, just as it was in Jesus' day-to-day life on the earth.

The opposite side of this is, a lack of the anointing will create a vacuum that is filled by a deception, a false anointing. When we shirk off the anointing, when we resist the Lord in the fires, we are left with "another" spirit.

"When all that generation had been gathered to their fathers, **another generation** arose after them who did not know the Lord nor the work which He had done for Israel." (Judges 2:10, **emphasis added**)

"But I fear, lest somehow, as the serpent deceived Eve by his craftiness, so your minds may be corrupted from the simplicity that is in Christ. For if he who comes preaches **another Jesus** whom we have not preached, or if you receive a **different spirit** which you have not received, or a **different gospel** which you have not accepted—you may well put up with it!" (2 Corinthians 11:3-4, **emphasis added**)

I have heard it taught that there is an alarming absence of true, biblical radicalism in the Body that we "well put up with...." I agree with this notion, and I think we need a return to radicalism in the Church.

I'm not preaching "radicalism" as some kind of militant jihad—this isn't some Crusade, "God wills it!" kind of talk. But I am arguing for radicalism from its origins: the Latin word *radix* means "root" (see some mathematical definitions)—the point of origin, the base, the springboard. Something that is fundamental and crucial, key, elemental.

The anointing is radical. And we are supposed to return to the roots of Jesus' power. This is a turning away from what is traditionally "normal," and making a radical shift in our "normal" viewpoints and establishments—breaking traditions and ritual conventions that are contrary to the anointing of Christ, and *our* anointing received from the hands of the Lord in the fires.

The Bible is chockfull of God's dealings with mankind—and they are all radically executed—the actions of Jesus on this earth is the prime (*radix*) example of this truth. In hermeneutics, christocentrism speaks of *everything* being centered in the works of the cross—any and every aspect of Christianity, singularly and as a whole, is supposed to be viewed through the death and resurrection of Jesus the Anointed One. This means that Jesus' radical nature and anointing was a product of being cross-centered. Not as only a means to an end—the ways and means we have of approaching God, through Christ's sacrifice (though this is of the utmost importance)—but also a *lifestyle*, a principle by which He lived and continues to live. We should live this way too.

Really, the Lord in the fires demands a radical abandonment to the cause of Christ from His disciples. "...The kingdom of heaven suffers violence, and the violent take it by force." (Matthew 11:12) So it is a radical Christian responding to a radical message that puts action to the anointing. Anything else is leaven. *Selah.*

I'm not trying to bash any one type of traditionalism in the Church. Not all pageantry and ceremony is *evil*, per se. But I am saying that any type of tradition that lessens or downplays the effective work of the anointing in today's life is dangerously close to presenting a gospel that is undermined by unreality, hypocrisy and compromise. A strong statement, to be sure. But that doesn't make it any less truthful. Left unchecked, the leaven of anti-radicalism yields extreme legalism and leads to carnality and sensuality.

I've heard it once said, "At the heart of the human problem is the problem of the human heart."

The definition of compromise is contrary to the definition of radicalism. It is conceding or capitulating a part of one's standpoint in order to come to terms with another. Taking a vital, basic belief and giving it up to maintain peace with another. To remain in the "comfort zone" of middle-of-the-road living. So you are either yielding to the doctrines of man, the doctrines of devils, or the doctrines of Christ (that's christocentrism!)

Notice the "buy from Me gold refined in the fire" passage of Revelation 3 is in the context of the lukewarm church. This leaven is a Laodicean spirit: "Because you say, 'I am rich, have become wealthy, and have need of nothing'—and do not know that you are wretched, miserable, poor, blind, and naked..." (Revelation 3:17)

Let me wind down this little subsection with an illustration from Numbers 32. So in preparation for the conquest of Canaan, Israel subdued the land east of the Jordan, then returned to the plains of Moab, camped beside Jordan opposite of Jericho.

Reuben and Gad (along with half the tribe of Manasseh) wanted to settle in the lands of Gilead and Jazer, which were not the promised land. Note that Moses became angry with them, accusing them of behaving as the spies had done in Numbers 13—when the Lord's anger was roused and He swore an oath that the original generation would not enter the promised land (save Joshua and Caleb.) Why? Because *they had not followed the Lord wholly.* That is the essence of sin, not following the Lord wholeheartedly.

Moses accused this new generation of also refusing to go forward. "Don't make us cross the Jordan." He accused them of discouraging the others from taking possession of what the Lord had promised to Israel.

The danger of their sin was a lack of radicalness. In fact they were seduced by a spirit of complacency and stupor, so content to remain in the comfort zone of a partial experience, a partial "win." This is at the heart of the antichrist spirit that is already in the world today. (1 John 4:3) It is a vain attempt to embrace Jesus apart from the anointing. It is an attempt to accept Jesus as the Lamb and not as the Lion.

Any spirit that is in opposition to the flow of anointing *now* is an antichrist spirit—it really is as simple as that. "... Having a form of godliness but denying its power..." (2 Timothy 3:5) Go back to that passage from 1 John 2 above, see that it is in the context of opposing an antichrist spirit. We know that the keys of the kingdom of the heavens is in the power to bind and loose (that is, the anointing.) (Matthew 16:19) Vain and empty imaginations (Romans 1:21; 2 Corinthians 10:5) reject everything that has to do with His anointing—though there can be degrees of rejection—still, an antichrist spirit rejects because it cannot *control* the anointing. And without that anointing, we're no threat to Satan's dominion.

So the gospel message is turned into an intellectual message, not a supernatural encounter. The antichrist spirit tolerates the mention of power (the anointing) as long as it's in the past; it works against faith in the now, and thus feeds off the residue of past moves of the Spirit. Again, I'm not bashing any particular sect of Christianity, but I am against antichrist Christianity (can you believe those two words are linked together?!) as a whole, and I bet you can think of a couple churches near you that subscribe to past anointing and shirk present anointing, or churches who have turned the power of the gospel into an attitude of the mind.

How can people who love God be offended by the anointing? It boggles the mind, but that is the essence of a religious, anti-radical spirit. We need to be set free from an acceptance of normalcy among our peers, released from what "they" think are religious norms of conduct, if we are going to experience Him and in turn be used by Him.

Look, I'm not advocating fanaticism here, people wigging out in the middle of praise and worship, barking at the moon in a chicken outfit—that's not the Spirit; that's either catharsis, mental instability or demonic. Yes, things need to be done decently and in order (1 Corinthians 14:40), but they need to be done! And let's be real frank here, not all things are being done that should be done, because so many of us don't want to ruffle any chicken feathers and shake people from their inertia. Apathy is one of the greatest enemies against the Spirit of God. The point of the Lord in the fires is to burn everything down to its radical roots, so thus the spirit of stupor is destroyed by the strong hand of the Lord.

HEAVENFIRE

WE NEED THE GLORY TO DESCEND, WE NEED THE anointing to bring freedom, a cleansing of sin to burn through the land—freedom from the power of sin is in the hands of the Lord in the fires. We need His fire to fall! The fire needs to come to the world, and it needs to come to His people. Rather than a spirit of stupor and antichrist, we need a spirit of judgment and burning.

Don't think that's biblical?

"When the Lord has washed away the filth of the daughters of Zion, and purged the blood of Jerusalem from her midst, by the spirit of judgment and by the spirit of burning, then the Lord will create above every dwelling place of Mount Zion, and above her assemblies, a cloud and smoke by day and the shining of a flaming fire by night. For over all the glory there will be a covering. And there will be a tabernacle for shade in the daytime from the heat, for a place of refuge, and for a shelter from storm and rain." (Isaiah 4:4-6)

"For by fire and by His sword the Lord will judge all flesh; and the slain of the Lord shall be many." (Isaiah 66:16) Of course I'm all about mercy and forgiveness and peace—don't misunderstand me. But let us not forget, in the fear of the Lord, that our God is a consuming fire. The words of our own Lord Jesus: "I came to send fire on the earth, and how I wish it were already kindled!" (Luke 12:49)

Fire can be a blessing in the heart of man, zeal ablaze within the bones. In fact, it is a promise of the Lord's: "For everyone will be seasoned with fire, and every sacrifice will be seasoned with salt. Salt is good, but if the salt loses its flavor, how will you season it? Have salt in yourselves, and have peace with one another." (Mark 9:49-50) Note this passage is juxtaposing heavenfire with hellfire ("For their worm does not die, and their fire is not quenched;" see Isaiah 66:24) There are two kinds of burning, you know? And tasteless salt is worthless, and fire that doesn't burn is useless. The point of this book is to let you know you *will* be seasoned with both, and they will do their work. But heavenfire is better than hellfire. (Boy, talk about stating the obvious...)

"And even now the ax is laid to the root of the trees. Therefore every tree which does not bear good fruit is cut down and thrown into the fire. I indeed baptize you with water unto repentance, but He who is coming after me is mightier than I, whose sandals I am not worthy to carry. He will baptize you with the Holy Spirit and fire." (Matthew 3:10-11)

The Bible is full of fire references—both kinds. But the good fire is what we're talking about. The pillar of fire, the tongues of fire. The type of heavenfire that is unquenchable, all-consuming, spiritually felt and seen. This kind of fire refines as it consumes; it illuminates, warms and protects from vicious beasts in the night. It is pliable, but it spreads uncontrollably and creates energy as it spreads.

Heavenfire will never lack for tinder and fuel, because *we* are the kindling, *we* are the brushwood. We are fanned by the flames, "not lagging in diligence, fervent in spirit, serving the Lord," (Romans 12:11) and stirred to confront the spirit of stupor and anti-anointing, just as Paul's "spirit was provoked within him." (Acts 17:16) His spirit was grieved and aroused to anger at the idols that had taken over Athens.

Indeed, "For the earnest expectation of the creation eagerly waits for the revealing of the sons of God." (Romans 8:19) So get on fire!

Just like Elijah asked, "How long will you falter between two opinions?" (1 Kings 18:21) He drew a line in the sand, "If I can prove to you the Lord is God, and not Baal, follow Him." And how is this proven? "...The God who answers by fire, He is God." (Verse 24)

You can't say you love Him and not obey Him. You can't say you know Him and treat Him as a pauper. You can't say He's Lord and leave His presence. You cannot shirk the fire of His anointing. Quit faltering and get to burning!

EMERODS

OUR LIVES ARE A GIFT, FIRES OF TESTING OR NOT. THE most loving thing the Father can do for you is to give you a divine slap of conviction on your spiritual wrist: you are to be a *happening*, not a space-filler. This slap on the wrist from the Lord in the fires is to awaken you to realize that your lifetime is the most precious gift you have been given. Yes, salvation is the *greatest* gift—but the very fact that you are alive is one of the most awesome things the Lord could give you, and one could argue you have to be alive in order to be saved!

What you do with your life is how you say Thank You to the Father for this precious gift. So, what are you doing with your life? Do you shirk the fires to avoid being taken out of your comfort zone? Or do you embrace the love of the Father as equally and fervently as the holiness of the Father? Do you love Him as much as you reverently fear Him?

I believe one of the greatest—if not *the* greatest—sins we can commit against God is to waste our lives, and regret is the cancer of life. He has planned something better for us (please take a moment to read Hebrews 11:32-40), and it is the refining fires that place us in a position a) to appreciate and understand His plan and b) to receive His plan in reverential fear and love and c) to execute His plan in holiness.

I've asked this question numerous times from behind the pulpit over the years. It's as appropriate today as ever it was. *What have we done with our faith?* What purpose has it served? You're not saved just to be saved (although, again, that is the greatest gift the Father has given.) But has our salvation *meant* something beyond our own benefit?

I am persuaded this generation must complete the race, the baton has been handed to us, we're the fourth man, and the Church as a whole is going into a divine sprint for the finish line. (That's a whole racing metaphor there to tie into moving from Hebrews 11 into Hebrews 12—I'm clever that way... *smile*)

A cloud of witness who went before us were refused to cross the finish line. This tells me, just as our lives are a gift, so is our faith a gift; and this begs the question: what kind of life should we live, knowing the people before us gave all for their leg of the race? There's no intimidation here, but rather inspiration.

I'm wholly convinced no one can say the Holy Spirit has come to them and just sit there and do nothing. No one can say, "I've seen God's beauty," and not worship Him with a sense of exuberance.

Even in the refining fires, we are not left hanging. Even in the midst of difficulties and trials, there can and should be a spirit of celebration. That is an aspect of the anointing from above, to create an atmosphere of jubilation—a table spread out for us in the midst of our enemy. (Psalm 23:5) The power of God awakens a celebration that swallows up the "party spirit" of the world—I believe our joy and jubilation make the world jealous. "How do you get so high?" they ask in wonderment. And there's no hangover afterward, to boot!

Really, it stems from an understanding of our identity in Christ; and whom He loves, He chastens (from Hebrews 12:6 and Proverbs 3:11-12.) The fires are not to burn us up, but to instill within us exuberant joy. That might seem like a contradiction, but it is the spirit of the world that is a spirit of intimidation—and our Lord has not given us a spirit of fear. (2 Timothy 1:7) Satan's priority is to make our existence seem futile, to make us feel unworthy. But the truth remains that the world has always been shaped by a handful of people, not the masses.

"... If My people who are called by My name will humble themselves, and pray and seek My face, and turn from their wicked ways, then I will hear from heaven, and will forgive their sin and heal their land." (2 Chronicles 7:14)

"My people" is an identifier. To do anything below what you have been created to do will leave you bound. So the Lord in the fires is not trying to burn you to a crisp—on the contrary, He is restoring the spirit of triumphant living. The *dross* of intimidation, fear and mediocrity is what is burned away—leaving behind the pure gold of a glorious, victorious, exultant life.

The baptism in the Spirit is a baptism into His confidence. The baptism of fire purifies, tests and refines that confidence until we are positively singing in the flames. "Now this is the confidence that we have in Him, that if we ask anything according to His will, He hears us." (1 John 5:14)

But note that God goes to "His people" first. When God judges the affairs of mankind, He first looks to see what "His people" are doing. Case in point, before the destruction of Sodom and Gomorrah, the Lord first went to Abraham. (See Genesis 18 and 19.)

After a particular fashion, Sodom and Gomorrah weren't destroyed so much because of what was going on in the cities, but rather they were destroyed because of what *wasn't there*. God couldn't find ten righteous people to save Sodom!

This tells me it doesn't take thousands to effect a change. It just takes some hardcore radicals, a revival core of people burning with the fires of conviction to say, "Give us this city, Lord." And of course, being baptized into His confidence is reliant upon the depth of God's commitment to us. But it doesn't take thousands—why, it can just take two:

"Then Jonathan said to the young man who bore his armor, 'Come, let us go over to the garrison of these uncircumcised; it may be that the Lord will work for us. For nothing restrains the Lord from saving by many or by few.'" (1 Samuel 14:6)

Jonathan sounds nuts, and his armorbearer sounds crazier than him! "Yeah, sure, why not; let's do what's in your heart." Those dudes were intense! And they're not the only ones.

The Angel of the Lord calls Gideon a "mighty man of valor" (Judges 6:12) while he's hiding out in the winepress threshing wheat. And again, it doesn't take thousands, it just takes three hundred, if they're the right group of people. Folks who bring the water up to their mouths, just lappin' it up—those who would not *kneel*, you know what I mean? (See Judges 7, if you don't.)

Moses is a little more level-headed. He sees this bush burning (there's fire again!) and asks, "Who am I that I should go to Pharaoh?" (Genesis 3:11) But the Lord's having none of that. "I will be with your mouth and teach you what you shall say." (Genesis 4:12)

Just as Moses stood in the court of Pharaoh with the name of God as his defense, so shall we stand in the court of the world system in these end-times.

Whatever your eschatology may entail, I think we can all agree that our understanding of the times will be directly influenced by the Spirit of confidence that is given in the fires. "End-times"—whatever that term may encompass—are for the elect's sake (that's supposed to be us, the elect.) Again, the end-times are not about fear and torture, something we fear is coming "some day"—you and I are to be a *happening* in the end-times. They are not to be a happening to *us*. We are not expected to be victims of a corrupt system, but to be world changers, tried by fire, ready to be used by the Lord as an apostolic, breaker anointing force.

This is why I believe there is a hastening of these types of fire encounters upon us. We are being primed, tested and refined, to be an expression in these "end-times." "But he who endures to the end shall be saved." (Matthew 24:13) This means *stand*, don't fall back—press our rights, execute a radical change in the fabric of society. All of this comes about because of our understanding of the anointing.

The anointing makes you a catalyst for power. A catalyst is an element that affects a change in everything around it, without itself undergoing change. World changers. Spiritual Rambos (that's deep.) How about "fire-lighters"? People that are radical in their confrontation against the enemy.

Let's take a look at Dagon. (1 Samuel 5) Now, to me this is just the height of idiocy. God will *not* share His glory with another. Period. Philistines steal the ark of the covenant, God's symbol of anointing on Israel, correct? Okay, stop right there. Rule #1: Don't steal the ark, all right? Look what happened in *Raiders of the Lost Ark*. I mean, how stupid can a people group get? Rule #2: Don't put the stolen ark in with an idol. Talk about a volatile combination. Let's do everything we can to incite the Lord's wrath, shall we?

And talk about the judgment of God, I can't think of a more wretched punishment. Whether it's bubonic plague caused by rats, or emerods (hemorrhoids) in the secret parts, the bloody flux (dysentery), the piles, or just plain ulcerous tumors, whatever—God is *displeased* here, you know what I mean?

(Not to put *too* fine a point on it. If you think I'm overplaying the graphicness of the plague, please note the Hebrew word was not permitted to be spoken aloud in the synagogue—they used the vowels of the word only—because it's considered vulgar, like spelling out a swearword. We're not just talking about a little upset stomach; we're talking about having the runs, okay? We're beyond Beano here; we're all the way up to Imodium.)

Dagon represents secular society. The ark is God's anointed, people who at any moment of time in history represent Him. When the anointed gets out of its place of influence, God is free to create (or allow, if that fits your theology better) whatever crisis is necessary to bring the anointed back to where it belongs—even diarrhea...

You cannot touch God's anointed and get away with it. Dagon will fall. Once you recognize *you* are God's anointed—tried in the fires until you're brazen as, well, brass—let's see society try to put you in *their* "temple."

God says, "Do *not* touch My anointed!" So much so He gives Abimelech an eloquent, tactful word: "You're a dead man. Don't you touch her, she's another man's wife. I'll take you and yours *out*." (Genesis 20:3) Something to that extent.

I've found that many times God forces society to arrange itself around God's anointed ones—His purposes and plans—to ensure there is a confrontation between what is right, and what is wrong. God's very black and white. If our secular, humanistic America hinders the work of God, He'll knock her down. Here's one point where I tend to agree with our current president: it's frightening to me to call America a "Christian nation." You know, it may not just be the sins of a unredeemed society that's to blame for all the world's tensions—it very well could be a backslidden, rebellious group of His own.

This is why I'm so alarmed at an ultra-grace doctrine that professes you've no need to repent of your sins once you get saved. You may not think our sins can cause these things, but we may be the reason for inflation, border troubles, rampant immorality. That's why there's the

Lord in the fires. His anointed ones don't always act very anointed. Not bashing people with an ugly stick here, just pointing out a truth; and I'm not missing the plank in my own eye, I'm just saying we need to get real and stop playing around with these dangerous teachings. Straighten up. No one wants hemorrhoids.

Or do you wanna be like Jonah, right? Follow me a second. Here's Jonah, wakes up, fishing brochures litter the top of his dresser, he's confessed to himself, "I am going to catch the *biggest* fish in history, man!"

God says, "I don't want you to go fishing in Tarshish—I want you to go to Nineveh, I'm about to wipe them out." (Probably with rats or another bloody flux...) God tells him, "You're My anointed one, My ark here. Nineveh needs you in the worst way."

"Uh-uh, Lord, I'm goin' fishin'. Got my lures, got my bobbers, I'm ready to go." And thickskulled man that he is, he flees from the presence of God (I mean, *really?*) and gets on a boat to Tarshish—which is *not* where God wanted him to go. So he's asleep in the boat, and God's mad, and He sends a storm that threatens to destroy the boat.

Now the sailors on the boat, they worship other gods, but they're not as dense as Jonah. They know someone has ticked off the deity, and the ship's captain starts chewing Jonah out: "Get up, ya bum, call upon your God. We're about to be sleepin' with the fishes."

The sailors drag it out of him: he's the reason God's so upset. They harangue him. "What have you done, you fool! How dare you rebel against God?" Now, I want you to note: whose sin caused the storm? The idolators? Or the backslider?

So they throw him to Jaws.

I've been using this joke for years, but I mean, seriously, can you imagine what someone would look like after being in the digestive juices of a whale (or whatever) for *three days*? Those hemorrhoids aren't sounding so bad right about now. No hair, no eyebrows, wrinkled white albino skin, looking like some kind of half-chewed raisin, ET-looking kinda dude. Just gets barfed up right on the shore.

God makes us look peculiar, to make us graphic, to bring about the needed impact to make a change. Peculiar is to be of a "different spirit" (Numbers 14:24), strange and unique. We're called a "peculiar people" in 1 Peter 2:19. The Lord revealed to me that peculiar in this instance means a heightened level of intimacy with Him—shut up and enclosed with Him in a chamber-like experience, face-to-face, heart-to-heart, life-to-life with Him. That kind of intimacy with the Father will make us look "strange" to others, in a good way—it makes us very attractive, because we get the people's attention. We need to quit worrying about being *acceptable*, and focus on being made inimitable by our intimacy with God—I maintain, we'll end up being more striking to others than if we try to be "normal."

Can you imagine what Jonah looked like, strolling into Nineveh, shouting, "Repent!"

Wouldn't you?

We need to wake up, Jonahs. People who've been in the fires won't hold their peace. It's time for the watchmen to rise up. We need to quit being "respectable" at the expense of the anointing. I mean, that is the nature of travail, you know? The point of the fires, the travail of our souls, is to open or broaden the way for a birthing to occur. God's anointing must pour forth. We can't stand in the way of that anymore than a secular society. Or we risk facing Jaws.

LEANNESS

THAT WHOLE "SUFFERS VIOLENCE" VERSE FROM Matthew 11 is really quite interesting, at least to me. I find in it an explanation for the massive moves of God on this earth, the revivals that throughout history have rocked entire people groups to their cores.

The whole "From the days of John the Baptist" phrase speaks to me of humanity's role in starting (and ending) a particular age. John was violent in his pursuit, and it shows me there is an *invasion principle* to revival. I think one of the purposes of the fires is to get us to an edge of "rawness" where we are not only *okay* with the intrusion of the Holy Spirit, the interruption of God's presence in our lives, but we are actively *seeking* His glory to invade us radically and mess up our worldview. We *want* to be "assaulted" by the forcefulness of the kingdom. I think we as the Body are starting to rethink what it means to be "in the Spirit."

It goes beyond just a "visitation"—not to demean a visitation in the slightest, any move of God is vitally important. But a total reworking of the wineskin of the Church, a renewal of blessing, a violent infusion of power. So, if John had a role in bringing about the new age of the kingdom, that tells me we too have a role in preparing a path and making the way straight for God's "next big thing."

If you don't think there is violence and fire in any major move of God, I refer you to Malachi 4:

"'For behold, the day is coming, burning like an oven, and all the proud, yes, all who do wickedly will be stubble. And the day which is coming shall burn them up,' says the Lord of hosts, 'That will leave them neither root nor branch. But to you who fear My name the Sun of Righteousness shall arise with healing in His wings; and you shall go out and grow fat like stall-fed calves. You shall trample the wicked, for they shall be ashes under the soles of your feet on the day that I do this,' says the Lord of hosts. 'Remember the Law of Moses, My servant, which I commanded him in Horeb for all Israel, with the statutes and judgments. Behold, I will send you Elijah the prophet before the coming of the great and dreadful day of the Lord. And he will turn the hearts of the fathers to the children, and the hearts of the children to their fathers, lest I come and strike the earth with a curse.'"

The Lord is basically saying here, "I'm not messing around." You've got Elijah represented by John the Baptist, heralding a shift of focus (note, I didn't say "throwing it in the garbage") from the Law of Moses to an era of Spirit and power. That's why Moses and Elijah are often mentioned together, the Law and the prophets pointing toward the culmination of Jesus Christ completing (fulfilling) the Law for us and ushering in an era of Spirit-filled power.

More than a visitation, but rather a *habitation* of conviction, love, peace and holiness. Which, let's be honest, is much better than being struck with a curse. The "turning the hearts" passage shows the connection between the generations, the two "covenants," so to speak, and it's these children and fathers that are the violent ones since the days of John the Baptist until now (which include you and me, because, uh, we're "now.")

All a "violent" person means here is one who is possessed of a vehement, eager, pressing, *burning* desire for something—in this case the manifestation of the kingdom. Simply put, the forceful push forward.

So when the Spirit is poured out (and poured out, and poured out) it is the violent, thrashing move of the people by their desperation to enter into the presence of God for freedom that marks the start of a new age in the kingdom. This kingdom power is fervently, enthusiastically, impatiently sought after and forcibly snatched at by these violent people. The people are burning for the manifest presence of God, and they take the kingdom of heaven by storm, forcing their way in.

The Greeks used the word *enthuses* (or *entheos*) which modernly has come to mean "enthusiastic." Its original connotation—which was often mocking—means "one in whom God is in" (not always relating to our God—but aptly applied to the violent Christians of the First Century Church, nonetheless.) It speaks of reckless abandon, possession, religious fervor bringing about a euphoric state of mind, effusion, to rhapsodize, to gush—yes, even to rave. The Latin *afflatus* carries a similar connotation, the concept of God blowing upon a person (inspiration, inspire.)

These *enthused* people are those who have an obsession to glorify God—really, those who desire to conquer kingdoms. That's why Christianity was considered so dangerous.

Who will God give His power to? An awakened generation of violent, enthusiastic people.

Jesus is at large; He isn't like anyone else. When He begins to move, it doesn't matter who's ready and who's not. When He gets in the mode to bless, He dismantles all concepts that hinder us from receiving.

So, one of the purposes of the Lord in the fires is to awaken within us our purpose—to provoke us to ravenous, violent hunger. Yes, of course, we have been blessed in the midst of this passionate pressure; God has restored. But we need to be asking ourselves, "Okay, we're violent, but now what do we do? What are we about? Where do we take this enthusiasm?" No one wants to be all dressed up with nowhere to go!

This kind of presence of God is the highest honor with which we can be associated. But we're not "zapped" *just* to be blessed. No, the point is to be around unsaved people with this kind of fervor, so that they turn to us and say, "I sense God is in you!" (That's enthuses.) We go through the fires in order to have that kind of zeal shut up within our bones that makes God *look large* to others, that magnifies His character and majesty to the world outside our own "clique" of fellow Christians. We exalt His personage to others, and they want to experience this enthusiasm for themselves. We are awakened so that we might awaken God to their understanding. As we increase in the awe of God, so shall they.

Except, oftentimes, we have exalted *our* personality in the church, not His. How often do our worship songs portray "God bless me" but not so much "God use me"? So there are a number of well-meaning Christians who have avoided the uncomfortableness of the Lord in the fires—whose fear and awe of the Lord is contained to a Sunday morning experience—and who have turned into a high maintenance, but low impact, group of people. Outwardly healthy looking, but with an inward emptiness, possessing the words of the Bible, the look of a Christian, but ultimately lacking depth.

That's not supposed to be a judgmental, critical statement, more of an observation based on experience. The good news is, we are being changed by the fires (sometimes whether we want to or not!) We are being transformed into a group that is not afraid of being used to enthuse the world around us. We know we're not here to have a good time (but a *great* time!) Determine in your heart to be promoted in the Spirit, to go through the fires of refinement, so that you might be taught how to *war* in the Spirit. Another reason for the fires is to awaken us to our need for a violent pressing of the kingdom.

Otherwise, we are left with people who have kept their morality, but don't have the spiritual fuel to fan them into a blazing flame. They've kept their light, but don't have their heat. And yes, they've kept their rules, but have disregarded their righteousness. And as I said earlier, tasteless salt is worthless, and fire that doesn't burn is useless.

They have a leanness of soul.

"They soon forgot His works; they did not wait for His counsel, but lusted exceedingly in the wilderness, and tested God in the desert. And He gave them their request, but sent leanness into their soul." (Psalm 106:13-15)

(Note just a couple verses later, "A fire was kindled in their company [those who envied Moses' and Aaron's authority.]" That's the *bad* kind of fire there.)

A person with a leanness of soul is a person who is satisfied with His partial presence, the partial expression of His character. And always, with a limited presence, one gets limited results. Leanness. I'm all about people receiving blessing and substance and prosperity, but we also have to cultivate a lack of satisfaction with where we are in God. Yes, satisfied, but also dissatisfied, you know? The only problem with people receiving, and always receiving, always receiving is it can create an indifference to the divine perspective of need—this goes back to the earlier concept of God *desiring* us, and us desiring God.

(Now, note, I'm not talking about receiving the necessities of life— people have to eat; having sickness and disease in your body is *not* you showing God that you understand the perspective of need, okay? I'm talking about a spiritual craving for His WHOLE presence—not paying your electric bill. God wants us to be blessed, but not focused on only material blessings. We're using Psalm 106 as a parallel for people who desire just enough of God to fill their bellies, but not enough to "eat of His flesh.")

The Israelites in their leanness were content to receive that which was just a substitute for the real need in their lives.

Leanness of soul creates a system of unbelief; it is a vexation of the soul. You want the wrong things, and it's never enough, no matter how much you receive them.

And not all leanness of soul is because of *our* wanton desire for the parts of God, and not the whole of God. We wrestle with a morally fallen society that is taxing to our spirits, and if we don't maintain a proper attitude of "going through the fires" to burn within us a correct passion for ALL of God, we can become polluted.

"...And delivered righteous Lot, who was oppressed by the filthy conduct of the wicked (for that righteous man, dwelling among them, tormented his righteous soul from day to day by seeing and hearing their lawless deeds)—then the Lord knows how to deliver the godly out of temptations and to reserve the unjust under punishment for the day of judgment..." (2 Peter 2:7-9)

Lot's soul was vexed. What does "vexed" mean? To be tormented by lots of little things continually, or sudden crises that rise up just to exasperate our lives. The great battlefield we war on is in our minds and emotions. Modern culture has created a monster with all its unbelievable pressures and disappointments. Without that solid anchor of hope that is only found in the complete presence of God in the midst of the fires, we can become disillusioned, disenfranchised, even deluded.

So one of the reasons for the fires, why we need to increase in the awe of God, is so that our *hope* might be awakened. We need to become possessors of a un-vexed spirit in this present darkness—the presence of God, with all its reverence and holy fear, can be an oasis in the desert for a weary traveler. A God-given presence to bask in that washes away the toxic effect of modern life. Possessing an un-vexed spirit means subjugating this insane world we live in to the order of God's kingdom.

"...They will take up serpents; and if they drink anything deadly, it will by no means hurt them; they will lay hands on the sick, and they will recover." (Mark 16:18)

This is the *opposite* of a leanness of soul. This is to be our portion, and this is one of the primary reasons we are being refined by the Lord in the fires.

LIGHTS AND GIFTS

FIRE GIVES LIGHT. JESUS IS THE LIGHT OF THE WORLD. (John 8:12) "In Him was life, and the life was the light of men." (John 1:4) He was given by the Father of Lights, and as we know, He only gives good and perfect gifts. (James 1:17) The "with whom" part of that last verse speaks, once again, of revealing God's unchanging nature.

"This is the message which we have heard from Him and declare to you, that God is light and in Him is no darkness at all. If we say that we have fellowship with Him, and walk in darkness, we lie and do not practice the truth. But if we walk in the light as He is in the light, we have fellowship with one another, and the blood of Jesus Christ His Son cleanses us from all sin." (1 John 1:5-7)

"We have fellowship," a connection with His life in the light. We know that Jesus' present day ministry is as our great Advocate in heaven, our High Priest, the Apostle of our confession. (Hebrews 3:1) His ministry expression gives us redemptive rights in the blood, which redeems and proclaims our fellowship with everything that is in the light of God. We lack for nothing because He translates and purifies our own words to bring heaven's commodity to earth. "If you ask anything in My name, I will do it." (John 14:14) Thus, our words become creative in spreading the kingdom glory. As we confess our association with the light of God, it becomes the ammunition for seeing the power manifested, because of how Jesus represents us to the Father—this goes back to the "partakers of the divine nature" from 2 Peter 1:3-4.

We are called to bear witness to that divine nature, and the Father honors our witness by sending His heavenly light to this earthly realm. He is faithful to all of His house, and in return He expects our honor and respect as the Giver of that light. So this is yet another reason why it is vitally important to develop a proper fear of the Lord, to increase continually in our awe of Him, and to work with the Spirit amidst the fires of refinement in order to develop this more fully.

The risk we run in not developing a lifestyle of godly fear and reverence is to cultivate actually a sense of revulsion—or let me soften that and say, a sense of aversion or indifference to the light of God and the gifts of His glory.

"But Jesus said to them, 'A prophet is not without honor except in his own country, among his own relatives, and in his own house.' Now He could do no mighty work there, except that He laid His hands on a few sick people and healed them." (Mark 6:4-5)

See, they wanted the Light to be a conquering King, establishing a physical kingdom to overthrow the Roman rule. But in reality, they were showing a disbelief in Him being sent as the "Spokesperson" of the Father. He didn't come in the fashion they were expecting; they had an extreme lack of discernment and were without a proper sense of honor (respect and reverence) for the Person God had sent. So they missed it—their opportunity to partake of the divine nature, and Jesus was restrained from doing any mighty work. Oftentimes God delivers His good and perfect gifts in a package we don't want. Why? Because the fires of refinement are supposed to bring us to a point wherein this fear of the Lord is hardwired into our spiritual DNA. I've said it elsewhere, in front of just about every sign, wonder and miracle, the Lord places an affront before it to force the people to make a decision: yield to His awesomeness or stiffen your neck and reject the gift.

We have to develop a discernment that is honed by the fires of refinement. It stems from our relationship with the Father; the more we get to know Him, the more we can perceive the authority He has given to those He sends in His name, starting with His only begotten Son.

So the anointing, in its own way, is a form of fire. As it flows forth, it burns away and lays bare the inward hearts and thoughts of the people, showing who is truly following God in reverence and awe, and who is hiding behind a façade of "fellowship with Him" that conceals a defiant and noncompliant heart. The anointing polarizes Christians as well as those in the world.

"Then Simeon blessed them, and said to Mary His mother, 'Behold, this Child is destined for the fall and rising of many in Israel, and for a sign which will be spoken against (yes, a sword will pierce through your own soul also), that the thoughts of many hearts may be revealed.'" (Luke 2:34-35)

So the fires burn away carnal thinking: that God's gifts must look a certain way to be welcomed. That God Himself must act or be a certain way in order for us to truly honor and revere Him. But the Spirit tests His children, pruning and purging them, bringing them to an understanding that in the level to which they receive the bringer of the gifts of the Father—Jesus first and foremost, but also meaning the ministers who come in the Lord's name—is the level in which they will receive the benefits of the gift itself. To be clear, the gift is the anointing with its myriad manifestations, be that in healing, prophecy, miraculous intervention, etc.

"And do not grieve the Holy Spirit of God, by whom you were sealed for the day of redemption." (Ephesians 4:30)

The Spirit is *the* Gift sent by the Lord, given to His followers. The point of increasing in our awe and reverence is so that we do not easily grieve the Spirit at work within us. That Greek word for "grieve" (Strong's #3076, *lypeo*, "loo-PAY-oh") means "to throw into sorrow" and stems from a root that can mean "annoyance" but also "mourning."

The Holy Spirit is in love with us; an intimate relationship exists between us. To dishonor Him is the same as a husband dishonoring his spouse (or vice versa) through an act of infidelity. That may seem like a strong statement, but I am thoroughly convinced that disrespecting the importance of the fire and the anointing operating in our lives is tantamount to spiritual adultery.

To reject His gifts, to downplay His anointing, to dishonor His presence, causes Him hurt and grief. Our sins of commission and omission drag Him down into the mire, creating a sense of mourning and annoyance, dare I say, even shock. Just as a spouse is *shocked* when they discover the unfaithfulness of their partner.

While being with the Lord in the fires may be an uncomfortable experience, one of the end results is to craft within us an abhorrence for shocking the Spirit.

The word "sealed" in the Ephesians passage above is *sphragizo* (Strong's #4972, "sfra-GEE-zo"), which speaks of God's approval, endorsement, recognition, affirmation, and sanctification, from the root meaning "something proven to be confirmed and authenticated." It can also connote being hidden or tucked away, something kept secret, like when a letter is sealed. The Father of Lights has sealed us with a precious Gift in the Person of the Holy Spirit. Therefore, whatever we do, let us stop grievously wounding that same Spirit and causing Him such intense emotional pain with our disbelief and sin.

"Or do you think that the Scripture says in vain, 'The Spirit who dwells in us yearns jealously'?" (James 4:5)

The original King James translates "yearns jealously" as "lusteth to envy." The Greek is *epipotheo* (Strong's #1971, "eh-PEE-pah-THEY-oh") and it's a compound word. *Epi* means "above" and *potheo* means "to yearn." So an intense, pressing desire, a supreme hunger or craving, yearning, pining for something. It doesn't necessarily connote a normal kind of hankering, since it can be translated "lust," to harbor a forbidden desire. A modern equivalent could define *epipotheo* as an addiction, an intense, abnormal and excessively aching yen.

The Spirit needs us, and all of His power and expression is directed at acquiring what He yearns for—that is us, only He knows why... *smile*

He's jealous and envious—this is Who we've been sealed with. A perfect, consuming Gift from the Father of Lights. So, He will bring the fire, yes; because He can't live without us. He's jonesing for us—and if that concept doesn't increase your awe of Him, I'm not really sure anything will.

So after a particular fashion, the supernatural expression in our lives, the signs, wonders and miracles, the demonstration of released anointing, is directly tied into our being sealed with the Spirit who is desperately desirous, and even jealous, over us. We're His; He wants us, and thus we are *marked* by the miraculous.

MARKED

YOU BECOME LIKE WHO YOU WORSHIP. THIS IS THE nature of an intimate relationship with God. And this is why I believe the release of the miraculous is so important. A demonstration of the supernatural—say, a gift of healing—is a sign of God's heart revealed, who He is on display. This is His very makeup and substance revealed, His very Person, not just a capability He has. And this creates the explosive revelation and astonishment that increases our awe and reverence of Him, cyclically drawing us into a deeper relationship.

The miraculous is a demonstration of not only God's authority, but His love also. That heavy hand of God, His glory and anointing pressing down on us, marks us, and we are to be marked by God's love so that a) we are brought into obedience to His will and b) brought into His glory. These two facets have been aptly entitled ministering out of His character (obedience) and ministering out of His presence (glory.)

So the signs, wonders and miracles are simply the marked imprint of being with God—His heavenly realm being brought into this earthly realm, the byproduct of an encounter with His Person—in the heavenly realm there is no sickness, right? So bringing that down to the earthly plane reverses sickness. In these encounters, we have a profound understanding that we are seated with Christ experientially, growing in a deeper personal relationship with Him, and thus we as an entire body are brought back into His perfect will. Again this is cyclical. Encountering His love, caught up in His glory, creates obedience, and obedience then creates more love for Him. We become more like Who we worship.

So the miraculous marks a person, but it must be reproduced, over and again—our awe "rubs off" on others, and they too become marked by the finger of God. More cycles here. The point of glory encounters, then, is for you and me to have a continual testimony of experience, and we can in turn open others to the Spirit—this is what it means to be "marked by God." We become a healer, because Christ is THE Healer. And we become like Who we worship, see? We're talking about ascending here, these glory encounters, increasing in the awe of God— the habitation of God, like we had discussed a little earlier.

This all speaks of access and acceptance, favor and blessing, seeing, hearing, discerning, *discovering* Who it is we worship. Intimacy with Christ is simply discovering Jesus in His anointing.

You know in Isaiah 11 where it talks about the Spirit of "counsel and might"? These glory encounters, these awe-increasing moments, are us standing in the counsel of the Lord—the face of God turned toward us, the working of the Holy Spirit within us, sharing His advice and plans to demonstrate the love of God to those around us. These are times when the Father of Lights says to us, "Here, I am sharing My heart secrets with you."

"But Jesus answered them, 'My Father has been working until now, and I have been working.' Therefore the Jews sought all the more to kill Him, because He not only broke the Sabbath, but also said that God was His Father, making Himself equal with God. Then Jesus answered and said to them, 'Most assuredly, I say to you, the Son can do nothing of Himself, but what He sees the Father do; for whatever He does, the Son also does in like manner. For the Father loves the Son, and shows

Him all things that He Himself does; and He will show Him greater works than these, that you may marvel.'" (John 5:17-20)

What's neat about all this, here, is that even though we must decrease, so that He may increase (we're talking about humility and humbleness being some of the greatest keys to experiencing these glory encounters—the sense of reverence and awe, right?)—even though we are less so that He might become more in us, it doesn't *dissolve* our own uniqueness. God made us special, each of us different for a reason, you know? But as you are marked by God, it allows you to be creative on your own part to express the miraculous through your uniqueness. You might express the Father of Lights differently than I would, but the miraculous effect is the same—a healing, or a sign and wonder, whatever it may be.

We are marked, sealed with the Spirit, because God has laid claim to us. We *belong* to Him, so He has set His ownership upon our foreheads, so to speak. (Read Ezekiel 9, Revelation 7.) This brings us full circle back to the concept of God's name being Jealous that was discussed earlier. It's fitting then, that we readdress this concept a bit more fully, outlining some of the issues we face when we reject God's jealousy, or rather disregard it.

MANURE AND TURPENTINE

THERE'S A STRONG CONNECTION BETWEEN DISEASES and idolatry, just as there's a connection between diseases and harlotry—you know what I mean? Not many people really talk about this in healing circles, so let's discuss, you and I. God calls idols "little dung heaps"—and giving our intimacy with excrement can mark us in a *bad* way. That's a strong image! Let your mind picture that for a second. *clears throat*

And the Lord can use this as a type of fire, refining us, but I would maintain this is a type of fire that is best avoided! It's always a good idea to stay away from burning manure. You ever seen someone make a bomb out of cow pies? Yeah, they explode, and they're messy.

Again, the idea is there are two types of burning—one is good, the other is ordure. So let's talk about the bad kind for a just a bit, and take this as an example of what *not* to do.

"So the Lord plagued the people because of what they did with the calf which Aaron made." (Exodus 32:35)

One of the hindrances we may have to receiving an awe-increasing encounter with the Lord—be that, in the name of healing or deliverance, further intimacy, whatever the case may be—can stem from being disobedient in "putting away the idols." In other words, one of the reasons why we may not be seeing a breakthrough, a miracle, in our lives may be because we have not "torn down the idols."

"Now it came to pass the same night that the Lord said to him, 'Take your father's young bull, the second bull of seven years old, and tear down the altar of Baal that your father has, and cut down the wooden image that is beside it...'" (Judges 6:25)

I trust you recognize I am speaking mostly to spiritual idols in this context—most of us don't have a wooden carving of Asherah on our mantles, and we're not burning incense to a fat Buddha out on the front lawn. But the concept rings true for spiritual idolatry as well as physical. We're talking about a heart issue here, making of something an "idol" that isn't necessarily an idol to begin with, deifying something that isn't godly from the start: "But then, indeed, when you did not know God, you served those which by nature are not gods." (Galatians 4:8)

Healing comes out of *faithfulness* toward God, not just *faith* for the miracle itself. The covenant of healing is rooted in obedience (Exodus 15:26), and faith towards God requires obedience, otherwise it's not really faith. If you're disobedient and "playing the harlot," you're being *unfaithful*, right? Like Hebrews 6:1 points out it's not just "repentance from dead works" but followed through with "faith toward God." Being *faithful* to Him, and Him alone, forsaking all others. "...Testifying to Jews, and also to Greeks, repentance toward God and faith toward our Lord Jesus Christ." (Acts 20:21)

It has always been this way with the Lord. He *will not* accept second place in any aspect of our lives—not even family. (Your homework assignment is to go read Matthew 10 for Jesus' teaching on the proper fear we are to have. I'll wait till you're finished.)

"And Jacob said to his household and to all who were with him, 'Put away the foreign gods that are among you, purify yourselves, and change your garments. Then let us arise and go up to Bethel; and I will make an altar there to God, who answered me in the day of my distress and has been with me in the way which I have gone.' So they gave Jacob all the foreign gods which were in their hands, and the earrings which were in their ears; and Jacob hid them under the terebinth tree which was by Shechem." (Genesis 35:2-4)

The Father of Lights, the Giver of every good and perfect gift, the One to whom we are ever-increasing in awe, could not make Himself any clearer:

"You shall not bow down to their gods, nor serve them, nor do according to their works; but you shall utterly overthrow them and completely break down their sacred pillars. So you shall serve the Lord your God, and He will bless your bread and your water. And I will take sickness away from the midst of you." (Exodus 23:24-25)

A condition of healing (the absence of sickness) is the total destruction of idolatry. Not just turning away from them, but burying them in turpentine. Follow me here for a second, okay? Terebinth trees. (Really, I'd say they're more like shrubs, but we're talking about Middle Eastern desert, so out there, they *are* trees.) They're related to pistachios, and they are the original source of the solvent turpentine. Incidentally, some people make a coffee-like drink out of it, but that's another discussion...

"Terebinth" is a translation for the Hebrew word *elah*, pluralized *elim* or *elot*. Sometimes it's rendered as "oak trees," but that's really the word *alon*, which is probably related. But I hypothesize, along with many scholars, that the root stems from pluralized *el*, or "gods." Also note—Exodus 15, Numbers 33—that after the Israelites left *Elim* (where in this context, we might infer a place of "tree gods") they came to Mount Sinai, a place of the *real* God, and soon after were making the golden calf. Interesting thought. Further still, David fought Goliath at the Valley of Elah. (1 Samuel 17)

And hey, as a free bit of marginally related trivia, there's an island near Narnia named Terebinthia, where the *Dawn Treader* was told not to make land because of a sickness among the inhabitants. Hmm. Idol worshippers? Perhaps Aslan had removed his blessing from their bread and water, and maybe Lewis was being intentional.

In either case, I would put forth that terebinth trees symbolize, or directly relate to, idolatry—the pluralized form of *el*. And there's biblical basis for this; see Isaiah 1:29.

We see in 1 Samuel, that an attitude of stubbornness is as offensive to God as an act of idolatry. The passage shows layers and layers of disobedience, leading to iniquity, and rebelliousness as odious to the Lord as sorcery and wizardry.

"So Samuel said: 'Has the Lord as great delight in burnt offerings and sacrifices, as in obeying the voice of the Lord? Behold, to obey is better than sacrifice, and to heed than the fat of rams. For rebellion is as the sin of witchcraft, and stubbornness is as iniquity and idolatry. Because you have rejected the word of the Lord, He also has rejected you from being king.'" (1 Samuel 15:22-23)

Idolatry is akin to spiritual adultery, just as pornography is a physical representation of lust and coveting after strange flesh—it fractures the soul and leads to iniquity. A shock to the Spirit, an offense to the Lord, the exact opposite of increasing in our awe of Him; it equates to the same as spiritual whoring. I recognize that's a strong statement, and I don't bandy it around lightly.

Idolatry can be of the heart and of the mind. Outwardly and inwardly, works of the flesh.

"Now the works of the flesh are evident, which are: adultery, fornication, uncleanness, lewdness, idolatry, sorcery, hatred, contentions, jealousies, outbursts of wrath, selfish ambitions, dissensions, heresies, envy, murders, drunkenness, revelries, and the like; of which I tell you beforehand, just as I also told you in time past, that those who practice such things will not inherit the kingdom of God." (Galatians 5:19-21)

"No one can serve two masters; for either he will hate the one and love the other, or else he will be loyal to the one and despise the other. You cannot serve God and mammon." (Matthew 6:24)

So the unlawful love of deceitful riches is idolatry, and it will consume the covetous person. Really, any pressing notion, vehement craving, that we entertain which does not glorify God can become idolatry. I've heard it said, "Any object of veneration that receives undue affection, whether abstract or material, constitutes a 'god.'" So if you become like what you worship, whatever you are spiritually, emotionally and physically intimate with becomes your reflection.

"And because lawlessness will abound, the love of many will grow cold." (Matthew 24:12) "Moreover the law entered that the offense might abound. But where sin abounded, grace abounded much more..." (Romans 5:20) Thank God, otherwise we're covered in manure and turpentine! Who'd wanna be with us then?

But seriously, we serve a jealous God who will not tolerate competition, and therefore, to increase in the awe of Him, it must be our stance that we will not permit any object of affection to steal our love away from Him. His zealousness over us, His Bride, His wife, causes His passion—His face turned toward us—to become intimately real, and we can't help but return that intimacy toward our only Love. The converse to that is He will reprove His people for their unfaithfulness.

"But Jesus perceived their wickedness, and said, 'Why do you test Me, you hypocrites?... "You shall love the Lord your God with all your heart, with all your soul, and with all your mind." This is the first and great commandment. And the second is like it: "You shall love your neighbor as yourself." On these two commandments hang all the Law and the Prophets.'" (Matthew 22:18, 37-40)

We're made in God's image, and to have any other gods is debasing, for us and for Him. And while I am persuaded that the Holy Spirit will continue to convict us as we permit Him to search our hearts for anything that vies for our attention on God, I believe that idolatry can be an inroad the enemy uses to plague us with infirmities.

Manasseh is a good example of this. (2 Chronicles 33) He's twelve when he takes over the throne (that's part of the problem right there) and does evil in the sight of the Lord; and in fact, he seduced the people to do *more* evil than the nations that God destroyed before the children of Israel—namely by placing an idol in the house of the Lord. Now, let's all say this together, once more with feeling, "This is a *bad thing* to do!" I predict hemorrhoids in the near future.

Not quite, but it's arguably just as bad. "And the Lord spoke to Manasseh and his people, but they would not listen. Therefore the Lord brought upon them the captains of the army of the king of Assyria, who took Manasseh with hooks, bound him with bronze fetters, and carried him off to Babylon." (2 Chronicles 33:10-11)

That's actually "nose hooks." (See 2 Kings 19:28.) So yeah, that's pretty bad. Now thankfully Manasseh wises up and repents, and the Lord restores him. But let's use this as an example of what *not* to do. Nose hooks are no fun.

"...And the Lord said to him, 'Go through the midst of the city, through the midst of Jerusalem, and put a mark on the foreheads of the men who sigh and cry over all the abominations that are done within it.' To the others He said in my hearing, 'Go after him through the city and kill; do not let your eye spare, nor have any pity. Utterly slay old and young men, maidens and little children and women; but do not come near anyone on whom is the mark; and begin at My sanctuary.'" (Ezekiel 9:4-6)

See, God's people are marked, those who sigh and cry over the abominations in His city. People who care about how the Lord feels, people who intentionally want to sigh and yield themselves to Him and His mandates. His decrees are always the opposite of abomination, you know? I wonder why it is so difficult for people *not* to stiffen their necks. It is a central component to the human condition, and it must be submitted and given over to the Lord.

Like I had mentioned in 2 Chronicles 30:8 earlier, the key is to yield and enter. We enter into the things of God only after we have yielded, and each yielding gives way to new enterings. (I don't think that's a word.) But you may have heard the term "bitter root judgments" before—these are the opposite of yieldings. (That's not a word either.) When we judge God, His Word, His messengers, we become bitter, and the root of bitterness carries its own judgment. If we don't yield, we cannot enter. Oftentimes it turns out that people just can't seem to give up the thing that's holding them back from increasing in their awe of the Lord—this is the judgment of a bitter root.

It's been my experience that the Lord must enjoy the process of measured, ongoing sanctification (yielding and yielding and continually yielding) as much as we *don't* enjoy it. That's the nature of the Lord in the fires—but He is fair; He knows us better than we know ourselves; and He always replaces vices with virtues. So, it's in our best interest, no matter how uncomfortable the process may be.

We need to rise above condemnation when we feel we have grieved the Holy Spirit. That's right, we need to yield up condemnation as much as the act that caused the grievance itself. Condemnation is a form of self-pity, which in turn is just a form of self-pride. That sounds incongruent, but it's true, if you stop to think about it. It's a pity party taken to an extreme level, designed to make us feel better about ourselves. We need to get rid of that, and in return the Spirit, who loves us, imparts an anointing that restores us to a greater sense of awe in God. So, don't fight the fires; work with them, is what I'm trying to say here.

LAND OF PROMISES

IN HIM ALSO WE HAVE OBTAINED AN INHERITANCE, being predestined according to the purpose of Him who works all things according to the counsel of His will..." (Ephesians 1:11)

I absolutely love that phrase, "obtained an inheritance." Along with the "exceedingly great and precious promises" of 2 Peter 1:4. Like the Israelites' promised land, the land of promises kept. Sadly, the spies (excepting Caleb and Joshua) were veiled in their understanding of just who God is to make these kinds of promises.

Really, though it *is* a sin of unbelief (read Matthew 11:20-24), it's also kind of a preposterous, even ignorant, stance to take: "because the land is so great, full of giants, how can we overtake it?" Only a great God could give so great a land. If He is who He says He is (see Numbers 23:19), then He wouldn't have promised it if He didn't have the ability to defeat the enemy. God has to be greater than the enemy, otherwise He isn't God, right? And God *is* great. Kind of a *duh* moment there to me.

But see, it's the iniquity of the people (stemming from an idolatrous heart.) Unbelief is the fatal flaw that comes from giving our love to something other than God. "So we see that they could not enter in because of unbelief." (Hebrews 3:19) While both are sins, there's a subtle difference between unbelief and disbelief. Unbelief means there's no value system in place, a basis for belief on which to build. Disbelief means, "I've heard it, I've seen it; I still refuse to believe it." It's willful ignorance, versus just ignorance. Yet God doesn't excuse either.

Like in the Exodus, each of the ten miracles, which were to be awe-encounters, was an extension of who He is, given to destroy the false images the Egyptians worshipped. Yes, it was judgment against idolatry, but it was also supposed to be a sign for them: don't be ignorant, here's the Real Deal, folks. You want to worship frogs? Fine, here's some *frogs*. What's that? You worship the Nile? Okay, here's some *water* for you. Oh, Ra's the sun god, huh? Watch *this*. Attention getters. True revelation of the greatness of His Person behind each miracle. (Yes, they were miracles *and* they were plagues. This goes back to the "affront placed before each sign and wonder" that I was talking about just earlier.) But poor Ramses II, God hardened his heart, and he just "didn't get it."

But hey look, I'm not beating up on the Egyptians nor the Israelites. We do much the same today, don't we? We often don't allow the previous moves of God to change us, just like they didn't. We often misinterpret His character, don't we? We often don't take Him at His Word, do we?

Like the Israelites, many of us have been (or are) in anguish of spirit, under cruel bondage, and we are thus **blinded by that bondage**. See, the Israelites were under a cruel yoke, not only being forced to make the bricks, but also had to gather the straw to make them. (Exodus 5) Troubles upon troubles. And their great labor under this spirit of slavery blinded them. Just like them, until we yield, and this governing spirit is broken, many people aren't able to believe and stay faithful. They've no willpower; they're stripped of self-confidence. Like robots, just lethargic and complacent. I've called it the "glaze of indifference" in other writings. Just like Israel, many people have a distorted view of God—they think leaving Egypt (the world) is coming out of one kind of bondage and heading into another—God is just another taskmaster.

One of the purposes of the fires (and no, we're not having to deal with Exodus 9 kinds of fires, thankfully) is to burn down barriers to the anointing, the awe-factor of God. Faith only operates where there is revelation. As we sigh and cry and yield, we *can* learn to believe things right out of our spirits, to discern those barriers hindering our awe-increase. We take God at His Word—He's not an insufferable tyrant (though He is firm.) He's a loving Husband and a Father. Yes, He wants to be obeyed, for our own benefit, not to cruelly shackle us under a different type of slavery.

"Watch, stand fast in the faith, be brave, be strong." (1 Corinthians 16:13)

I've taught in other materials that the above verse carries the connotation of keeping one's shoulder pressed to the wheel—while the original King James' "quit ye like men" is specific for the masculine gender in the Greek, the notion applies spiritually to men and women equally. In other words, I know Paul is telling men to be manly, act like men and "be strong!" here; but the concept we're speaking of, the imagery I'm trying to convey, is that we all need to learn not to jerk our shoulders back from the work before us.

It's important to work with the Lord in the fires so that when He reaches out to us, we don't allow our unbelief or disbelief to keep us from reaching back to Him for liberty. We don't pull our shoulders away from Him; we acquit ourselves like "men" (whether we're boys or girls) by being strong in the faith, standing fast, knowing God's goodness pervades everything in our lives. We need to develop buff spiritual muscles. (The Greek verb in "be strong" implies an act of our own will even though it is a command, and it means to grow stronger continually.)

God's not using the fires to enslave you. It's easy to bear His ark with His Spirit's help. But He needs us to respond properly, because like the Israelites, if God can't use us, if we don't yield, our carcasses can be left in the wilderness of unfruitfulness. This is sad.

I've said it before, it's like some Christians only want to experience the supernatural upon their deaths—so that it's, like, something out of their control. To experience the supernatural here on earth demands some kind of response. Boy, I'm serious here, we can't let fear, bitterness, religiosity, doubt, traditions and institutions of men, hinder us from responding to the Lord in the fires. We need His presence, we need His living Word.

"Rejoice always, pray without ceasing, in everything give thanks; for this is the will of God in Christ Jesus for you." (1 Thessalonians 5:16-18)

Dear readers, this is a command; it is the will of God for us. When we are pressed and tested, refined in fire, even in elements of suffering—though, as we'll see in the next section, it's important to note that much of our sufferings are self-inflicted—we must learn to give thanks always. Why? Because we want to achieve a greater ability in the Lord to put up with more difficulties and adversities? No. But rather, because we remain steadfast in the faith of God's goodness, that He is incapable of changing that aspect of His nature any more than He is capable of changing His holiness toward us. See, even if our troubles are *not* His perfect will (and more often than not, they *aren't* His perfect will—God has no delight in our suffering), by yielding to the Lord in the fires and trusting in His goodness, rejoicing always, praying without ceasing, giving thanks continually, God will "use" the elements of refining fires to change *us* (not Himself) into something more like Him.

He never moved. It's us who moved around Him, and He permits testings and trials (whether they were His intention or not) to get us to a place where we understand that His goodness toward us never alters.

I ask that you take several minutes and dwell upon these above paragraphs and then proceed into a short discourse on "suffering."

Suffering vs. Suffering

THE POINT OF THIS BOOK HAS BEEN ABOUT THE FIRE OF God coming down, heaven fire falling and consuming us, burning away the rough edges of "self" so that the Lord may burn through you more brightly. It has not been your traditional book on "intimacy with the Lord" nor "fear of the Lord," though we have discussed these topics. The main thing that I want you to take away from this book is that testings and the refining fire are to release a greater revelation of God's glory and power in your life and in your ministry, in whatever capacity you serve the Lord. This book is intended to bring out just a couple concepts surrounding the fire of God that will help to increase your awe of Him, and therefore, help spread that awe to others.

So, this book is not about "suffering"—and yet, I don't think a book about baptism in fire would be complete without at least addressing the subject of baptism in suffering. I'll start off by saying I think we have to be careful when we bandy around phrases like "Christians are forced to suffer" or "Christians must endure misery." Not because I wholly disagree with the notion of Christians suffering—that would be simply ignorant. But these are often polarizing statements that don't lend much leeway, or rather, they don't fully define the concept of "suffering." From a certain standpoint, Christians will suffer, that's obviously true. They suffer the reproach of Christ (Hebrews 11:26) and He is our great Example, "for though He was a Son, yet He learned obedience by the things which He suffered. And having been perfected, He became the author of eternal salvation to all who obey Him..." (Hebrews 5:8-9)

"For this is commendable, if because of conscience toward God one endures grief, suffering wrongfully. For what credit is it if, when you are beaten for your faults, you take it patiently? But when you do good and suffer, if you take it patiently, this is commendable before God. For to this you were called, because Christ also suffered for us, leaving us an example, that you should follow His steps: 'Who committed no sin, nor was deceit found in His mouth'; who, when He was reviled, did not revile in return; when He suffered, He did not threaten, but committed Himself to Him who judges righteously..." (2 Peter 2:19-23)

First, there needs to be clear distinction between following His example in His sufferings, but not in His substitution. We must distinguish between the example of Christ in suffering and the substitution of Christ in suffering.

In His life He was spoken against, reviled, persecuted. We can expect similar things for raising a Christian standard in our lives, for it is a matter of dying to self (which is the point of being with the Lord in the fires.) But when it comes to dying for sin, the shedding of blood, Christ took our sins and sicknesses upon Himself as our Substitution— in this area, He suffered so that we wouldn't have to.

A lot of our trials and tribulations are self-inflicted from making bad decisions or acting in rebellion; they're not "God-inspired." I am of the particular belief that physical sickness and disease is *never* authored by God to teach us about Christ's suffering. God does not "make" people be sick. That does not exclude the Lord working through a particular circumstance, even if it wasn't His will for the person to undergo the circumstance in the first place. But I think it's very safe to say God doesn't give someone cancer to teach them something about His Son's suffering, you know?

I think we have to be careful when we arbitrarily declare someone's suffering as a result of sin, or a result of following Christ's example. It takes a level of discernment, and we'd be wise not to judge one person's mishaps as, "Well, there must be a sin issue in his or her life." Neither can we just patently declare the suffering as "*from* or *for* God."

But with all that being said, there is an element of Christian suffering that is to be expected.

"Therefore, since Christ suffered for us in the flesh, arm yourselves also with the same mind, for he who has suffered in the flesh has ceased from sin, that he no longer should live the rest of his time in the flesh for the lusts of men, but for the will of God. Beloved, do not think it strange concerning the fiery trial which is to try you, as though some strange thing happened to you; but rejoice to the extent that you partake of Christ's sufferings, that when His glory is revealed, you may also be glad with exceeding joy." (1 Peter 4:1-2; 12-13)

Christ suffered humiliation. When He laid aside His rights and privileges to operate as God, becoming a Man, He gave up a certain rightful dignity and glory. Why did He do this? "For in that He Himself has suffered, being tempted, He is able to aid those who are tempted." (Hebrews 2:18) We cannot say that God just doesn't understand what we are going through.

Christ suffered weakness of the flesh. That doesn't mean He was ever sick (He wasn't)—but He uniquely understood the frailty of flesh by becoming Man, so that He could identify with us, and yet all without sinning Himself. This way we could come to Him, knowing He would be gracious and merciful because He recognized what it was like to be fully human, all the while still remaining fully God.

"For we do not have a High Priest who cannot sympathize with our weaknesses, but was in all points tempted as we are, yet without sin. Let us therefore come boldly to the throne of grace, that we may obtain mercy and find grace to help in time of need." (Hebrews 4:15-16)

Okay, so that's God, but what about other mortals like you and me, other Christians who suffered?

"So they departed from the presence of the council, rejoicing that they were counted worthy to suffer shame for His name." (Acts 5:41)

Paul lays it out as only he can: "But in all things we commend ourselves as ministers of God: in much patience, in tribulations, in needs, in distresses, in stripes, in imprisonments, in tumults, in labors, in sleeplessness, in fastings; by purity, by knowledge, by longsuffering, by kindness, by the Holy Spirit, by sincere love..." (2 Corinthians 6:4-6)

What's all this mean? Paul's speaking about trials, tribulations, times of leanness, suffering lack, anguish, confinement, disorder, commotions, sleeplessness, being "worn out" sometimes, being unsettled, mistreatment, burdened, tested, even physical assault. He goes on to outline personal things he underwent in 2 Corinthians 11:23-30. In other words, he oftentimes had it pretty rough...

But through it all: "The Spirit Himself bears witness with our spirit that we are children of God, and if children, then heirs—heirs of God and joint heirs with Christ, if indeed we suffer with Him, that we may also be glorified together. For I consider that the sufferings of this present time are not worthy to be compared with the glory which shall be revealed in us. For the earnest expectation of the creation eagerly waits for the revealing of the sons of God." (Romans 8:16-19)

And for what purpose do Christians suffer? Again, I defer to Paul: "We are hard-pressed on every side, yet not crushed; we are perplexed, but not in despair; persecuted, but not forsaken; struck down, but not destroyed—always carrying about in the body the dying of the Lord Jesus, that the life of Jesus also may be manifested in our body. For we who live are always delivered to death for Jesus' sake, that the life of Jesus also may be manifested in our mortal flesh. So then death is working in us, but life in you." (2 Corinthians 4:18-12)

He admonishes Timothy: "If we endure, we shall also reign with Him. If we deny Him, He also will deny us. Yes, and all who desire to live godly in Christ Jesus will suffer persecution." (2 Timothy 2:12; 3:12)

The point is, *these* kinds of sufferings are intended to settle us, mature us, "...if indeed you continue in the faith, grounded and steadfast, and are not moved away from the hope of the gospel which you heard... I now rejoice in my sufferings for you, and fill up in my flesh what is lacking in the afflictions of Christ, for the sake of His body, which is the church, of which I became a minister according to the stewardship from God which was given to me for you, to fulfill the word of God..." (Colossians 1:23-25)

Just knowing the Word and walking by faith won't necessarily "perfect you in the faith." "But may the God of all grace, who called us to His eternal glory by Christ Jesus, after you have suffered a while, perfect, establish, strengthen, and settle you." (1 Peter 5:10)

See, many Christians buck against adversity, simply because they don't understand the concept of trials by fire. They refuse to stay in a difficult situation, and so they prolong their agony. The concept of the Lord in the fires is lost on them. We would all do well to follow Jesus' example once again: He was *led* by the Holy Spirit in the wilderness. And after He had suffered "a while" He returned in the power of the Holy Spirit. (Luke 4:14)

Jesus Himself promises persecutions and tribulation in Mark 10:28-30 and in John 16. But the good news is, "These things I have spoken to you, that in Me you may have peace. In the world you will have tribulation; but be of good cheer, I have overcome the world." (Verse 33)

Now, not all trials and testings and tribulations are the result of being with the Lord in the fires. The single most common instigator of difficulties in our lives is ourselves. Bad decisions, sowing and reaping dumb behavior. None of us are above this, but hopefully as we mature and grow in the Spirit, we see less and less of self-inflicted misery. Even these kinds of trials the Lord can turn around to serve a purpose, bringing us to repentance and leading us into changing our ways, though He never intended for us to have to go around the mountain the hard way.

Another proponent in trials and sufferings comes from those around us. Other people's dumb decisions can affect our quality of life as well. Again, this isn't what God desired, but it is something He can utilize to bring an entire people group into a greater understanding.

Sometimes it's the enemy of our faith, the Accuser himself, who sends trials of fire. How you can tell a trial is demonically inspired is whether or not it can be explained by natural means. So, if you break your foot because you were foolishly climbing up a rickety ladder in the dark in the middle of a thunderstorm, well, that might not be the devil. That might just be because you did a pretty imprudent thing. However, when it comes to physical attacks, money draining that can't be explained because of bad financial decisions, mental harassment that isn't the result of something self-induced, rocky relationships where you can't identify a source of the contention—these quite possibly could be attacks of the enemy.

And yes, sometimes trials and tribulations are ordained by God. But this is a slippery slope to walk up. Christians often try to put all the blame for their difficulties off on God: "Well, the Lord is just really trying to test me." Possibly. But not always. We need Spirit-led discernment and judgment before we arbitrarily attribute a certain trial to "coming from the Lord." Or some may say being "permitted by the Lord." In either case, the Bible makes it clear God takes no pleasure in tormenting us. (Isaiah 63:9; Lamentations 3:33) But sometimes, yes—just like in real life, if a son or daughter is being particularly bullheaded, not yielding to a gentle rebuke—the Lord will use other means to chasten, discipline, correct or reprove us. But take Hebrews 12:5-6 in light of Psalm 32:8-9. A lot of the "God-authored" trials and tribulations are direct results of the first cause for discomfort: ourselves.

Also worth noting, the Lord does not *tempt* (James 1:13), He *tries* or *tests*. He *must* know that we love Him over all else, but He doesn't lead us to sin. A lot of unenlightened people cite Abraham offering Isaac as a sacrifice unto the Lord as some sort of wonky "proof" that God is malicious. But of course, if they bothered to study the account, they would see that God never had any intention of letting Abraham murder his own son—even though in the future, the Father Himself wouldn't spare *His* own Son, which is the foreshadowing signified by God providing a substitute for Isaac. See Hebrews 11:17-19.

Okay, so what's the point of being refined in fire? To build resolution, diligence, persistence and grit. (See James 1:24 and Romans 5:3-4.) So we become tempered like steel, folded over and over again, honed to a fine, sharp edge. So we don't fold under pressure. To bolster and increase our faith. (1 Peter 1:7) To give us an eternal perspective on things, so we are not always looking at the present. (2 Corinthians 4:17-18)

Ah, what about Job? Right? Probably the oldest book in the Bible, not a very happy tale, at least until the end. Well, first, you and I are *not* Job. They don't read about our trials and tribulations thousands of years later—we're not included in the canon of scripture. I'm not underestimating or downplaying what you may be going through; I'm just saying that we probably ought not to equate our difficulties with Job's unless we are implicitly clear on this from the Holy Spirit, anymore than we would equate our sufferings on the same level as Christ's. I daresay 99.9% of us as Christians, especially here in America, have never had it as "bad" as Job, or Paul, or Peter, or our Lord. But, that doesn't mean there isn't something to be learned from Job's trials— otherwise it wouldn't have been inspired by God to be in the Bible.

The fact of the matter is, the Lord was glorified at the end of Job. His goodness and mercy overshadowed the sadness of the story. (See James 4:10-11.) Whether it was a "thing I greatly feared" (Job 3:25) or whether the Lord was permitting Satan to test Job as an example for all of us coming later, the truth remains that God is looking to work all things to our good and deliver us from our burdens. (See Jeremiah 29:11.)

FIREBOLTS IN BRAZIL

To CLOSE THIS BOOK, I WANT TO SHARE WITH YOU AN experience of heavenfire. I share it to encourage your faith, because I am firmly persuaded that the Lord in the fires is refining us so that we might become more like Him. And in return, He will entrust to us encounters likes this. I do not exaggerate when I say this was one of the greatest signs and wonders I've ever seen manifested on earth. This is what we are all pressing into, what we are all wanting to see amplified in our lives, and I hope this book has helped in a small way to increase your awe in the Lord.

But first! Just to make you wait with anticipation, let me insert a quick teaching that fits well here. I want to tie it into the concept that the Lord confirms His Word with signs following. (Mark 16:20) Not the other way around. I see many well-meaning ministers try to get this out of order, and the results are usually limited. God does nothing apart from His Word, and as we place the Word first, then the miraculous follows closely on its heels to prove the validity of that Word.

Now follow with me here just a couple paragraphs: Habakkuk 3:15 is an interesting verse, "Before Him went pestilence, and fever followed at His feet." What in the world does this have to do with the Lord in the fires? The word "pestilence" in the Hebrew is *deber* (Strong's #1698, "DEH-var") and it comes from a primitive root that is taken as "a word" in the sense of destroying something by speaking. To speak a word of command that puts to flight. It can mean to threaten, to promise, to sing, to declare, or to converse. In some Greek translations, "pestilence" is replaced with *logos* (the Word.) I don't have the space in the context of this work to expound fully on *logos*. If you don't know, go read *Aletheia Eleutheroo*.

The word for "fever"—translated as "burning coals" in the original King James—is the Hebrew word *resheph* (Strong's #7565, "REH-shef"), and it actually means a "firebolt." Flames, sparks, burning heat, coals— it's translated as "hot thunderbolt" in Psalm 78:48 and as "arrows" in Psalm 76:3. So, to burn feverishly as if on fire. To be inflamed.

How cool is that? Or, I mean, how *hot* is that?

The correlation I want to draw here is the Word is followed by the fire. Not in reverse order. When the Word is preached, it is confirmed by heavenfire from the Holy Spirit—that is, signs, wonders and miracles.

Okay, so now on to my testimony. You thought I'd forgotten, huh? (I did actually. My mind was all feverish after that last little freebie.)

In all seriousness, it was in the early Eighties that a terrible tragedy struck a famous evangelist, one who had been commissioned by Aimee Semple McPherson to establish Foursquare churches in the country of Brazil. Over the course of his ministry, this evangelist had held major revivals there and had helped to establish hundreds—maybe thousands—of churches. Truly a wonderful man, who was sadly robbed and murdered while in a parking lot in Los Angeles. Just horrible.

His grieving wife called me to ask if I would be open to taking over his Brazilian crusades that had already been set up. Of course I agreed, and this became my first overseas trip. I can't remember the exact number of cities we went into; I think it was twenty or twenty-two, but we were there for six weeks. As I recall the smallest venue had about five hundred attendees, the largest maybe fifteen or twenty thousand.

You need to understand that at that time, the country of Brazil was under a classical Pentecostal view of Christendom, which is not a slam at all, but most of the Christians were very strict in their dress, what women could do or not do in the name of ministry, so on and so forth. I mention this because at the time most of the Christians had a viewpoint that one had to tarry and wait upon the Holy Spirit in order to receive the baptism with the evidence of speaking in tongues. When it was God's time, and after enough prayer and fasting, the Spirit in His set time would infill the believer subsequent to their born again experience.

Now, while I believe we're more illuminated in this day and age concerning the baptism in the Spirit, I want to say that I do not think it is wrong for some people to wait upon Him like that. Some heart preparation and a certain understanding of just what a person is receiving in the baptism is in order—after all, it *is* being baptized with the Holy Spirit *and* with fire (Matthew 3:11), the point of this book! Often prayer, fasting and tarrying can produce some wonderful results for people who struggle with the infilling of the Holy Spirit. But there is also an element of truth in the kingdom of heaven being *now* and praying for the baptism with understanding, receiving it by faith, and having an expectation to receive a heavenly prayer language at that time.

But during this overseas trip, the Lord impressed upon me that my entire message for the whole six weeks would never get out of Acts 2. I was told to teach on nothing but the baptism in the Holy Spirit with the evidence of speaking in tongues at every single session. So I did. Some of these crusades were on neutral grounds, and some services were held in massive churches. Generally at the churches I would encounter a situation where the pastor, his family, and perhaps a few associates were baptized, but most often, none of the people in the congregation were. It wasn't so much the pastoral staff bucking against getting the people baptized, it was usually a case of them not knowing how to lead them into it.

So over the course of the trip, teaching out of Acts 2 and nothing else, we led thousands into the baptism. Perhaps tens of thousands, I don't know a realistic estimate. Let me just say, a whole, whole lot. Entire congregations baptized all at the same time *en masse*. It really was a remarkable experience just to see that! God loves to set His people on fire!

I've since learned that many of the young people who were baptized in the Spirit during those crusades are now some of the greatest pastors and leaders in Brazil, bringing the people into a greater charismatic truth, freedom and experience. Praise God!

Okay, so on to the sign and wonder. One of the cities early on in the six weeks, I'm preaching Acts 2:3-5 to probably a couple thousand people. What was mind-bending was that every time I made a statement regarding the baptism, the people would rush the stage, surging and pushing forward. It was the pull of the Spirit, so strong on them that they couldn't *wait* to get to the altar and receive His gift. But the problem was, with a crowd that sized, a pitching sea of people, it was becoming a safety issue. People could easily get trampled and hurt. I couldn't finish the message. Every sentence I spoke produced a crushing throng of eager, desperate Christians.

We'd try to reestablish some kind of order, get people back into their seats, and after the next sentence, here they'd come again. If you've never seen a couple thousand folks try to rush you all at once, I don't know if you can truly understand the experience, but let me just say, it's unnerving and unsettling.

I said to the Lord, "You're going to have to protect us here, we might get mobbed!"

And so the Lord did. Now, this wasn't *just* for our sakes—He could have stilled the crowd in any number of ways—but the Lord wanted to show His people a sign and wonder, a truly singular occurrence that proved the validity of the Word being preached. Heavenfire.

As far as I know, *everyone* saw and heard this. As I'd finish a proclamation of the Word, the people would surge forward, and the Lord would send down bolts of lightning to strike on the concrete floor. This was visible and audible to the natural, naked eye. Indeed, the Lord made flashing clouds. (Zechariah 10:1) A firebolt would strike the ground and knock the people back, slain in the Spirit. I'd speak another word, they'd rush forward, and another bolt of lightning would shower down in front of them, driving them back to the seats or sending them sprawling.

Can you imagine when those people got filled with the Spirit? I'm here to tell you, folks, the Word is backed by the power of God, His heavenly fire, and as we yield to His burnings, the Lord in the fires will *make sure* your awe is increased in Him!